Praise for

We Over Me

"Khadeen and Devale Ellis's story shows that marriage can be a bumpy ride, but if you can laugh and cry together, argue fairly, and put *we over me*, you'll be on your way to long-lasting love and commitment."

—Tiffany "The Budgetnista" Aliche,
New York Times bestselling author of *Get Good with Money*

"Putting *we over me* is a concept that we have applied to our relationship for twenty-five years. Khadeen and Devale are great examples for how loving, playful, devoted, and business-minded your relationship can be. We are certain their testimony will inspire you and activate your relationship to mirror what they model."

—Dondré Whitfield and
Salli Richardson-Whitfield, actors

"This book will have you laughing and crying, and it's a must-read for couples and singles who want the best out of their relationship (or who just want to be entertained)!"

—Tommy Oliver and Codie Elaine Oliver,
founders of Black Love, Inc.

"How grateful we are for Khadeen and Devale's impact on our lives through their courageous transparency in the practice of love. *We Over Me* teaches us that it is their love for themselves, each other, and their family that invites us all to love and love more abundantly."

—KAREGA BAILEY and FELICIA GANGLOFF-BAILEY, PhD,
SOL Affirmations podcast

"Khadeen and Devale are a true example of what marriage is and how the foundation is *love*—from the highs to lows, ups and downs, and everything in between. *We Over Me* unpacks the core values of defining your own marriage, while keeping the commitment in the forefront. This book is a must-have and is sure to help tons of people and their marriages."

—EVA MARCILLE, actor

"K&D give hope to millennials who want to follow their dreams, remain in love, and have families. Staying married in this day and age takes a whole different mindset, and this book gives an intimate and honest look at the inner workings of their strong union."

—GIA PEPPERS, award-winning journalist and television host

We Over Me

We Over Me

The Counterintuitive Approach
to Getting Everything You Want
from Your Relationship

Khadeen and Devale Ellis

with Leah Lakins

RODALE

NEW YORK

Published in the United States by Rodale Books, an imprint of Random House, a division of Penguin Random House LLC, New York.

Rodale & Plant with colophon is a registered trademark of Penguin Random House LLC.

Originally published in hardcover in the United States by Rodale, an imprint of Random House, a division of Penguin Random House LLC, in 2023.

ISBN 9780593577622
Ebook ISBN 9780593577615

Printed in the United States of America on acid-free paper

RodaleBooks.com | RandomHouseBooks.com

9 8 7 6 5 4 3 2 1

Book design by Andrea Lau

To our amazing parents:
Karen, Troy, Sheron, and Morrison.
Because of you, we are who we are today.
We love you, and thank you for everything.

Contents

We Over Me

Introduction

We would like to start this book by stating that there is no perfect way to exist in this world. In fact, we'll take it a step further and say that *no one* has unequivocally figured this thing out. We are all in search of this mythical place called "Happily Ever After." Yet, we all find ourselves part of one big social experiment called life. With that being said, we as people don't owe each other anything other than the space to exist freely. So when it comes to relationships, everyone has the right at any point to say, "This really isn't working out for me in a way that is advantageous for all parties involved, so I'm going to move forward in a different direction."

Not exactly how you thought this book was gonna start, huh? You thought it was gonna be a list of how tos and we don'ts. Sorry, but this book is not that at all. This book is about choices. Specifically, the individual choices that led to a blessed union we are very proud of. It's about learning to respect the perspective of the one your heart so desperately wants to control. This book is about learning to love yourself so much that you learn to love someone else the way you always wanted to be loved in the first place. We know that was a mouthful, but trust us, we'll explain. Throughout this book you will learn more about us. Not as an example of how you should live your life, but as an example of how we built the love we have to live the life *we* want. Welcome to our love story.

Even though we share our lives on social media with millions of people, we certainly do not consider ourselves to be a celebrity couple. What we strive to do, along with sharing our highlight reels, pretty pictures of our children, and stories of triumph, is show some of the grit and real trials that arise in our relationship. Hence the reason why you are holding this book in your hands. We pride ourselves on being raw and transparent about what a healthy relationship looks like to us. The main thing we've learned along the way is that a "healthy" relationship does not come in one form. The secret to a healthy relationship *for you* will never be found on the pages of any book. This book is an entertaining way for you to experience how we discovered what worked for us, and hopefully prompts you to get curious about what works for you. The secrets for what will work for you can only be found in *you*.

We like to try to find the humor in a situation, but our

relationship isn't shits and giggles all the time. We are committed to putting in the actual work to make our marriage and our family thrive. We have our moments, and we never want people to look at us as a perfect celebrity couple. We wrote this book so that you can find your own path toward happiness in your relationship.

Ultimately, in a relationship, you have to ask yourself, "Am I willing and in a position to serve the other person?" Too many people go into relationships thinking about what they can gain from another person. Women have their lists of things that they're looking for in a man or men will be seeking what a woman can bring to the table. People have unrealistic ideas and expectations of what they need a person to have; meanwhile, they aren't bringing a fraction of that. If you're trying to get with someone who makes six figures, is handsome or beautiful, and is a go-getter, but you're not any of those things, how do you expect a healthy and equal relationship to work?

Instead of focusing on what you can get, turn that around and declare, "This is what I am bringing to the relationship and this is why I could be of value to someone. I am looking to be a partner. I am looking to elevate. I am looking to grow. I'm looking to build a legacy with someone." These are the goals you need to focus on if you want to grow or rebuild your relationship.

If you are aspiring to be in a relationship, you have to be transparent about what you want, show up as yourself, and leave the representation of yourself at home. That false self is not going to get you far. It can't last. It's not authentic. You need to show up as yourself and be confident in who you are. If you're not confident in who you are, work on yourself first. Stop going into relationships broken, jaded, tainted, and tattered. If you aren't willing to do the work on yourself first, all you are going to do is project that unhealthy behavior on to someone else.

Our desire to have a healthy relationship stems from seeing far too many unhealthy ones. Those unhealthy relationships that we were exposed to on a regular basis have made the two of us determined not to end up that way. Even as married adults with children now, something will happen between our parents and we will look at each other and say, "We CANNOT be like that."

Khadeen

Fairytales are a legit setup. By now we should all be tired of the hopeless romantic story about the damsel in distress who is desperately waiting to be saved by a strapping, princely gentleman. The guy who sweeps her off her feet and hoists her out of her current circumstances of destitution and poverty. We tell this story over and over to make ourselves believe their happily ever after, as they ride off into the sunset. The end. Roll credits. Right?

Little did we know that life actually commenced after the

fairytale ending. This was a surefire way to set us all up for failure when it came to marriage and relationships. Now is it possible to achieve your own version of a happily ever after? Absolutely. But what they fail to show was the grunt work necessary to achieve this seamless, mystical lifestyle. And still, regardless of the work and time invested, nothing is ever quite so smooth—particularly when attempting to unite two individuals who are aiming to live purposefully in their truths, all while trying to be considerate of each other.

I have heard in the past that love should be easy. For the most part, it actually is. Who doesn't want to bottle up that new, lusty, in-love aura and take a swig of it every now and again to relive that euphoria? The "love should be easy" jargon leads one to believe that intimate connections should flow without a hitch in order for them to be worth it. That's cute, and yet again, another foolish falsehood. On the contrary, relationships require real labor and effort, regardless of the type. The difference between a relationship with a parent, child, or another family member is that these are typically nonelective relationships. You have no choice about who you were born to or who you birth. In a work environment, you are required to coexist and work amicably with others based on the common goal of the business or company.

The nice thing about friendships and in most cases of romantic relationships is that these are connections where you choose to become involved. For the most part, friendships flow seamlessly because you naturally have common interests, likes, and similarities. It's truly a beautiful occurrence when someone's energy is enough to make you want to be around them frequently. Now throw a little razzle-dazzle, attraction, and lust into the mixing bowl and you have some batter that is good enough to make anyone want to lick that bowl. In spite of that, it's only the beginning.

I admire people who know off the bat that they are not relationship or marriage material. It takes a noble person who is self-aware enough to know that they are not equipped to coexist with another human being. If more people were honest about that, it would save so much heartache and confusion because you are not entering into a space where desires and intentions are misconstrued.

You have to be in love with the notion of marriage, not in love with a person. Now, finding your person is indeed a substantial part of the equation, but a person can and will change. Marrying for the person puts all the onus on that individual and ultimately is not fair to either party. What happens when he or she has a bad day or week? What do you do when life starts *life-ing* and shit ain't as sweet as it once was? Do you throw in the towel when that person no longer contributes to your overall happiness? Marriage is signing up to being on a team where submission to the overall greater good and goals of the family supersedes any solo mission.

I always knew that I wanted to be in a relationship. For as long as I can remember, I desired marriage and kids. I remember attending various cousins' weddings over the years as a kid, and I would daydream about what my wedding day would look like and who I would be meeting at the altar. I would get close enough to the bride to feel the tulle from her dress against my skin or practice the first kiss on my arm after the officiant pronounced us man and wife. My groom was faceless at the time, of course, but he was someone I knew who would reveal himself one day.

Had I not been married or romantically involved with someone for the past two decades, I believe that I would have been a serial monogamist. I enjoy the company of another person, but juggling men would not have been my thing. No shade to people who do, because sometimes juggling is required to figure what you like and dislike. At the same time, I definitely feel like I missed out on that dating phase of life. I always envisioned that I would be living the *Sex and the City* moment—a young, working, career woman who had her own place, would come and go as she pleased, and date casually. I also intended on settling with someone who, too, had his fair share of relationships. I wanted to be with someone with his wild oats sowed and all, so that when the time came he would know, without a shadow of a doubt, that I was the one. I lucked out with Devale, although I think my route was more arduous.

In my case, I was forced to learn who Khadeen was in my late teens and early twenties, while simultaneously attempting to be considerate of the feelings of a man my age who was also trying to do the same. This was a potential recipe for disaster—and trust us, we have definitely had those disastrous moments. There was a mental and emotional divide that had me in a chokehold. The divide was me learning about myself and tending to the needs and wants of someone else. My love for my relationship oftentimes clouded my logic when it came to what was ultimately best for me, and even Devale.

Many single folks I've spoken to, some of whom are divorced and back in the single dating scene again, have referred to dating as a cesspool of egos, facades, judgment, and uncertainty. But quiet as it's kept, us married folks have our fair share of such activity. Shit ain't always sweet and we will unpack some of that in this book. The good, the bad, the highs, the lows, the crescendo of breaking points, and the willingness to mend. When I look at the world today, I often think about what could remedy so much of the hurt, pain, evil, and trouble that exists. I would like to think that if everyone was able to experience the kind of love Devale and I have, this planet would indeed be a happier place. I know that's saying a lot, but there is nothing like being able to tackle life with your equal—someone who is along with you for the ride but will also make their own pit stops along the way. Some days, it's almost like getting into the passenger seat of the vehicle, starting a route to a common destination, knowing good and well that maybe you should've taken the other exit, but you go along silently for the ride knowing that you trust and believe you will still end up in the right place.

I would love for other couples to experience the kind of bond Devale and I have. It's often hard to sum up into the appropriate words. But if you will imagine with me for a moment—it's like walking into your favorite Jamaican restaurant and you're craving an oxtail dinner. Not only do they have the oxtail tender and ready, they also have rice and peas, and the server smiles while not being stingy with the portion, *and* gives extra gravy without asking. That's me and Devale, heavy on the gravy. Despite our differences, disagreements, and everything that we've been through, I love the shit out of that man. We're determined to do life together and there is no other option for us. In the past when we've broken up or struggled through hard moments, we would throw around the word *divorce*. But now that word is not even on the table. We know that we're willing to work on whatever it is we're going through in that moment because divorce is not an option and disagreements are temporary.

Forget everything you've heard—marriage is a service-based industry. If you are not up for that task, don't even bother. As we've begun to shift our focus on serving each other and finding ways to make each other's lives better, this mindset has helped us to navigate our goals and our relationship more efficiently because we're so much more intentional about making sure that the other person is in the best space to tackle whatever may come his or her way. Focusing on serving Devale is a practice that I am continually learning and improving on with each passing day. Some days I'm spot-on, and others, I fall short. There is a humanness when we try to allot grace because life always has a way of showing up and it forces a natural shift. Before, our focus shifted to service. I would wake up, start running down the to-do list for work, family, self, and others, and go full speed into asking, "What deadlines need to be met with our content creation?" or "What do the kids need to do after school?"

But now my mindset has repositioned itself, and the day starts more easily by being curious about how I can be of service to Devale and make his plate a little lighter. Focusing on serving each other has helped us so much with just navigating our respective goals and keeping our relationship healthy. The fact that we haven't really seen many healthy relationships is a driving force for us to set our own couple goals. We create what we want to be our own version of a healthy relationship.

Our goal for you as you are reading our story and learning from our lessons and mistakes is that you can begin to determine how to have a healthy relationship that is built on a foundation of love, service, partnership, and legacy. You do not have to fall into these relationship stereotypes about marriages falling apart after the birth of the kids or marriages collapsing after an infidelity. We've been through those valleys and then some. We are living proof that you can have joy and peace in your relationship if you are willing to put in the work to create your relationship on your terms. It is just imperative that you are forthcoming with yourself, as an individual, and with your significant other, because there is no room for lack of lucidity in any relationship.

Devale

People think a healthy relationship is the image that a couple chooses to show to the world. Social media has provided a place for people to curate their love story. If you see a couple who appears to be perfect, you most likely will assume that their marriage or relationship is healthy and ideal. In reality, that couple who you are idealizing may not be in a stable, healthy relationship at all. The worst part about social media is not the fact that people are trying to fool others. The truest complication is that they don't even realize they are fooling themselves.

When I was growing up, my parents always presented a unified front. They not only presented this image to us as their children, but they were careful to maintain that image in front of everyone else. While my parents never argued in front of other people, they would make passive-aggressive digs and comments to each other. Some people would believe that the kind of relationship my parents had was healthy because they kept their arguments private and maintained their peace.

But what I saw from the inside out was how toxic those passive-aggressive comments were to my parents' marriage. While they were good at hiding their disagreements from other people, it was difficult for them to communicate when no one else was around. The people that my parents were trying so hard to front for would have been shocked if they heard the truth of their private conversations. And here is the crazy part, I would consider my parents' marriage ideal to any standards—even today.

I started to realize that this behavior wasn't unique to my parents. When I looked around at other family members and the parents of my close friends, everyone appeared to be happy on the outside. But then when they got behind closed doors, that's when the truth about everything was laid out.

For me and for so many of my peers, we'd never truly seen a healthy marriage when we were growing up. The truth is that we had to learn for ourselves that a healthy marriage is transparent and allows plenty of room for open communication. It takes time to understand that a marriage that makes room for honest communication isn't toxic or abusive—it's one where each partner has room to grow.

Khadeen and I have had people make wild comments about the kind of real and open conversations that we have about our marriage on our platforms. People expect us to be offended or angry at each other instead of realizing that it's that level of communication that keeps our marriage going and growing. Khadeen and I have agreed to accept honest communication as the foundation for a healthy relationship.

If you're lucky, you have a good best friend who will tell you when your breath stinks or if you forgot to put on deodorant that day. A true friend would never let you walk around smelling like you played full-court basketball just because they don't want to hurt your feelings. Sadly, most of us tend to call that type of friend a hater because we have all been conditioned to view honesty as hate. So even if you have someone in your life who doesn't like telling you the truth, I'm sure you try your hardest to hold on to that relationship. It's natural—we as humans typically want to hear what makes us feel good as opposed to what is good for us. So when it comes to romantic relationships, we tend to stay in relationships that may not be healthy but look good on the outside. We put on a facade. If you want to be in a healthy relationship, be willing to have real, open communications and stop comparing yourself to other couples. When you compare yourself, you're always going to fall short of what you think is the ideal relationship.

We tend to ask everyone else what they're looking for so that we can present these unrealistic goals to our spouse as opposed to asking our partner directly and accepting what they have to say. Once you ask that question, you may not like the answer. But once they've given you their answer, then it's up to you to make the choice of whether you want to work within the realm of their needs and wants and be of service to them.

If you're looking for a healthy relationship, start focusing on your partner. Ask your partner honestly what they need and what they desire in a relationship—and then listen to their answers. Be open and honest about what you need and what you want. That is the best way to truly find out what a healthy relationship is—FOR YOU.

When you turn the final page of this book, I want you to know that you have what it takes to be the kind of partner that you want to be in your relationship. I want you to be empowered to know that you can come back from a knock-out fight, a bankruptcy, an abortion, a failed business, or any other kind of disappointment that you can think of and still build a good relationship that you can be proud of. Khadeen and I have been through all the scenarios I just mentioned (and more!), so we know what it means to choose each other when life gets hard. We know how to love each other on the days when we don't like each other. We're not here to be your relationship gurus—we want to inspire you to find the right answers in your relationship and create the love you want.

Chapter One

Don't Be Afraid to Make Your Own Rules

Some of the biggest challenges that we hear from couples is that they're trying to follow somebody else's blueprint to create their love story. People are so caught up in trying to look like or be the perfect "couple" that they don't take the time to figure out what's really important to them and what values they need to start their relationship off on a solid and stable foundation.

We started our love journey together in our late teens, so there were more than a few times that we were speeding down the freeway of love with no brakes in sight. While we felt that we were young and invincible, life showed up real quick and let us know that we weren't that special and that we could easily get knocked upside our head with a few bruises and scrapes along the way.

But even with all these twists and turns, the thing that we

continue to be proud of is that we created our love based on our own rules. Khadeen was the first one to initiate intimacy in our relationship, and at one point she was the breadwinner in our home as Devale was beginning his acting career. And Devale was the first to be bold enough to pivot into his dream of becoming an actor after walking away from his career in the NFL, which then inspired Khadeen to chase her own goals as a makeup artist, an on-air TV personality, and social media content creator.

Coming from families that looked successful on the outside but were actually emotionally dysfunctional behind closed doors, we knew we couldn't follow the old marriage playbooks from our parents. We had to create our own rules about how we wanted to communicate, build, and thrive together, and create a family that we could be proud of. Some of these rules that we created for ourselves were broken and rebuilt time and time again. Some of our primary values about serving each other and propelling each other's goals have remained the same.

If you are truly committed to having a lifelong relationship that is able to withstand the challenges that are sure to come your way, you have to be willing to step away from everybody's opinions and make your own guidelines. We know that there are still people following rules like observing ninety days of abstinence at the beginning of a relationship, shunning women for embracing their sexual autonomy, taking on those old Mars vs. Venus rules from the 1990s, or feeling like you have to let a man be an alpha male and take the lead. No shade to anybody if these classic approaches work for you. But we have a good feeling that they probably don't, so how do you create a dating vibe that works for you? How do you step into your own sexuality and sensuality without guilt, judgment, or shame? When is the right time to define your relationship? Who gets to say "I love you" first—and does it even matter?

So let's talk about what it means to start off on the right foot in creating a good relationship and help you find the value in creating your own rules.

Devale

The biggest lesson that I learned immediately from our first date was to say exactly what you mean and what you feel. If you're dating with purpose, when you first meet someone and you're getting to know them, it's important to tell them exactly what you want, what you need, and how you feel. That is the best way to make sure there are no blurred lines. Don't worry—if they're the right person, you won't scare them off. You'll be setting the boundaries for healthy communication going forward.

After our first kiss, I told Khadeen straight up, "I do not want to be anybody's boyfriend." I was *super* glad when she replied, "That's fine, because I wasn't looking to be anybody's girlfriend." We knew we both liked each other, and we were both curious to figure out exactly what that was going to look like. We were both upfront and transparent with each other. With all my eighteen-year-old's confidence I said, "I don't know exactly what I want, but I know that I like you."

That step was important for me because throughout our marriage, I've learned that sometimes you don't know exactly how to articulate what you want or need from your partner, but you can start by articulating what you want for yourself. From there, the choice is up to your partner to oblige you and decide if they want to serve you in that capacity.

As Khadeen and I continued being honest about what we wanted individually, our relationship continued to grow and the foundation to get stronger. Even if we didn't agree on what we wanted at the same time, at least I knew what she wanted for herself, and we made choices to serve each other in that capacity. We made mistakes, of course, but having that solid foundation made it easier for us to be honest and reevaluate what was working and what wasn't.

DEVALE'S HOT TAKE
Giving Your Partner Grace

Give yourself and your partner grace with all the changes that happen during the course of your relationship. Don't give up on your relationship because it doesn't look like the ones you see while scrolling through your timeline.

Feeling lost and misunderstood early in a relationship is completely normal. Being deliberate about how you communicate and seeking to understand each other is the only way to truly find common ground.

Khadeen

All those rules you've heard about from him, her, them, or read in Dating 101—forget them. The dance that was supposed to be a synchronized, melodious tango has morphed into that TikTok of somebody's aunt trying to do the latest routine. It's off beat, slue-footed, and out of date. One of the big things that I learned from approaching Devale first was that you can't be afraid to shoot your shot. In full transparency, I didn't march up to him on the first whim. I was a shy teenager who would admire him from afar on a few chance meetings.

I remember seeing his family in the audience when I was emceeing the spring festival at our old elementary school, Bethlehem Baptist Academy, one May circa 1993. At the time, Devale had transferred to another school but his sister still attended Bethlehem Baptist. From the stage, I maneuvered around the spotlight to scan the rows to see if he was in attendance, but no luck. I also happened to work summer school as a student counselor and was placed in his sister's class one summer. I would ask Tori almost everyday if Devale would be picking her up. Poor Tori never knew I was asking just to get a glance of my boo, who didn't know he was my boo just yet.

And then there was the handful of times I would go to Kings Plaza Shopping Mall with my cousin and best friend, Sophia, to see if Devale was behind the Haagan-Dazs counter next to the infamous Cookie House. I ignored Sophia's nudges to just go and buy some ice cream because I was just too nervous about potentially being in conversation with him. What would I say? What would he think? At the time, small talk wasn't my forte and nerves completely got the better of me. It's like I was a ghost follower before ghost following was a thing. One day in particular, I purposely got cute and talked myself into going for it at his workplace because "why not?!" I did all that just for him to be off that day.

But I also knew that those "chance meetings" weren't really chance because we went to rival high schools and seemed to have at least two to three degrees of separation. It just had to be the right time, because your girl was definitely plotting. When I talk with my single friends who are looking to date, so often there is a rigidness that some have when it comes to pursuing or being pursued. It's almost as if the stars, moon, constellations, and flavor of the month at Nothing Bundt Cake all have to align in order to crack a smile or say hello.

I have a friend on the dating scene who made a great connection with a guy and they exchanged numbers. He told her straight off the bat that it would be a little while before he could call her because he was in the process of starting a new job. But she just waited for him to call or text, and she became more frustrated and angrier the longer she waited. I told her she should go ahead and make the first move, but she insisted that she didn't want to come across as thirsty or desperate. GIRL! Shoot your shot!

I said, "Sis, how do you think I got Devale?" I've always tried to encourage my friends to forget about those traditional dating rules. If there's someone that you see out there who sparks some interest, say hello. Come up with a funny or clever segue to spark conversation because quiet as it's kept, men like to be pursued as well. That "thirsty" mentality is immature and dated. Go for it in that moment because you just don't know when you'll have that chance again. Making that choice to take a chance can be the catalyst for copping your boo. Let that sink in.

Devale

When I met Khadeen in August 2002 at the Trey Whitfield banquet, I was an honoree and she was the emcee for the evening. My first thought was "Damn, she fine as f*ck!" and she was wearing a crown, so I was really intrigued.

When she first came up to me and said my and my brother's names, I didn't know that she had this whole plan in her mind that she was going to come and try to holler at me. I wanted to be around her because the whole event was a lot of boring speeches and everyone was dressed in tuxedos and gowns. The whole ceremony wasn't my thing. The honorees and the emcee were placed in a different holding room for some time, so it gave us a chance to get to know one another.

I didn't have a plan or a divine epiphany that this was going to be the woman I was going to spend the rest of my life with. I just thought that she was pretty, and I was curious to see how it would play out. Before she left, she snatched my program booklet away from me and said, "Since you ain't gonna ask me for my number, I guess I'll just write it in your book." Then she wrote her number in my booklet. But little did she know I was just playing it cool like my uncle Kev taught me. I was going to ask, but I guess she couldn't wait.

Khadeen

Getting ready for the banquet, I had to make sure everything was perfect. After all, I did scam the invitation and saw the name DEVALE ELLIS in bold under the list of 2002 Academic Honorees. I said to myself, "Oh, he's smart, too," after already knowing he was a star football player for Madison High School. I was a booster for Madison's rival Midwood High School and he would single-handedly smoke our team with back-to-back touchdowns. It was a formal event, so I had to wear some sort of gown. I also knew that I would be wearing my Miss American US Teen crown and banner and that was enough to get attention. I remember asking my mom to go shopping for a new gown and she gave me the "Chile, please" look and told me to look through my closet. Me? Wear a dress for the second time?! I cringed at the possible fashion faux pas but obeyed my mom and looked through it. I decided on this cute, sexy coral asymmetrical wrap dress that I wore when I competed in the Miss Jamaica US pageant months before. It was a hot August day, my tan was popping, and I felt like a million bucks.

I walked into the banquet hall and greeted some familiar faces on the way in. Low-key, my eyes were scanning the room till I finally saw Devale standing off in the distance with his brother, Brian. This was my chance, and listen, nothing makes you feel more confident in a moment than looking and feeling your best. It was again like that moment on the pageant stage for the first time. Hands clammy, knees weak, and anxiety through the roof, but take a deep breath and remember who the eff you are. I knuckled to myself at my thoughts and walked over to, in my mind, my future and his little brother. "Devale and Brian Ellis," I blurted out. "My name is Khadeen. You probably don't know me, but I went to Midwood High School and I used to see you play for Madison." I figured I would hit him with the football correlation because I knew how guys felt about their sports. I told him that I would be helping out with the awards and stuff and I'd see him around. Now I had to walk away. I turned and felt his eyes piercing me through my back as I walked over to the cocktail-hour and buffet stations. I ate daintily in case he was watching. We ended up together again backstage, casually talking until the event started. It was a good time and he received a small scholarship from the foundation.

As the event began to wind down, his mom took a photo of the two of us and I just knew he was about to ask for my phone number so he could keep in touch. But nothing. Everyone was saying their goodbyes and we were finally out at the valet stand. I was questioning so many things in my head at the time, like "Was I too much?" and "Maybe he's just not interested." I felt like my "move" was in vain. But I had to make one more attempt. I went to say a final farewell and playfully took his program booklet out of his hand. "Since you were too shy to ask for my number, I'm just going to write it in here for you." We both laughed and he flashed me a smile in the way only Devale can. He wrote his number in my program booklet and we parted ways. Me with hopes that something would come of this time well spent. Devale mentioned that he was heading to Hofstra in the fall. On the car ride home, I'd be lying if I didn't say a part of me thought, "Man, what would that look like for me? What would that look like for us if I did actually end up at Hofstra?" But it would be another two months before we finally did link up.

Devale called me a few times during that summer after the banquet. He wanted to hang out and, truthfully, so did I. But his advances were usually met with my sister, who was eight at the time, aloofly hitting him with "She's not home" and hanging up on him. When I did pick up the phone, I had to say, "I'm so sorry. I'm on my way to Indiana" or "I'm on my way to Maryland."

That summer before I met Devale, I had just won the Miss New York American United States Teen title. After winning that title, I knew that I would have to go on to the national competition, where I would compete against all these girls representing the other forty-nine states. At that pageant, I won the national title, which was a great honor for me. But it meant I had to do community service work as part of my title duties.

I was also working on another path at the time as a choreographer. My dance background helped me out and I was traveling to a couple of different states pretty much every weekend, getting paid to work as a choreographer. That was my summer job at the time, and my way of making money. This was one of the reasons why I was super busy and not able to connect with Devale that summer. But I can't say that he wasn't on my mind because I would definitely think of him, especially if I heard that he had called or I got a message from my sister or my brother that said "This guy named Devale called." At the time, I just thought, "Oh, I'll get to him eventually."

Devale

I started calling the number she gave me, and every time I called, her little sister, Sakari, would answer the phone and say, "Khadeen's not here!" and hang up. So, at that time, I thought Khadeen was curving me. I thought, "All right, well, this just wasn't meant to be." I also started thinking back to what everybody was telling me all summer—that I should keep my options open when I get to college. I knew that we had this great connection, but I didn't know what to do. I was just focused on being a football player at that time, and I wasn't trying to be anybody's boyfriend. I kept my head focused on getting into Hofstra because I knew that once I got to college, the sky would be the limit, and that's what I was ready for.

I would also be lying if I didn't tell y'all that I was all into another young lady at the same time. This young lady and I met earlier in the summer and grew extremely close. If I wasn't training for football or spending time with my homies, I was with her. But Khadeen's forwardness intrigued me. The other young lady was younger than me and everyone was telling me that I should leave all my high school love affairs behind because college was filled with *grown-ass women*. Not gonna lie, I was excited about that, plus I saw Khadeen as my first opportunity to experience a *grown-ass woman*. Khadeen was already in college and working, so I felt like tappin' that (that's Brooklyn slang for sexual intercourse,

FYI) before I left for school would be a major notch before I got to campus.

Too bad it never happened. Khadeen was too busy and I felt like I was too poppin' to keep chasing some chick that pretty much forced her number into my book. That's what I told myself to get over the thought of being rejected. Don't judge me. I was eighteen years old and drove a 1989 Nissan Maxima with black rims, a red light underneath, and a twenty-inch subwoofer in the trunk in 2002. *Fast & Furious* was the hottest movie out at that time, I was a Division 1 scholarship athlete, and I could bench press 225. I *was not* about to be trippin' over no girl. So I left her alone.

Khadeen

A month before our official first date on October 3rd, we saw each other as we were picking up our little sisters from the same school. When I saw him, I was like, "Oh my God, Devale! I can't believe that I dropped the ball all summer and never saw him." And then around the same time, I saw him with some chick on his arm and I said, "Wait a minute—I didn't know he was dating anyone. I gotta find out what's really going on!" It could have easily just been a friend or a family member. But when I saw him with a girl, I was intrigued.

I went home and scrambled to find my program booklet from the banquet. I damn near tore my whole basement apart looking for it. My mom was clearly bewildered by my frantic state, but I never divulged to her what exactly I was looking for. That evening, the pageant director called me for an appearance at the Leukemia & Lymphoma Society's Light the Night Walk at Hofstra. My heart suddenly dropped when she said Hofstra and I knew this wasn't just happenstance. I felt even more of an urge to reach out to Devale. Of all places to have this Light the Night Walk, it was at Hofstra and I knew it would be crazy to go all the way there and not at least say hello. After my failed attempts at finding the booklet, I racked my brain to figure out a way to find him. Pre–social media age, it was a bit of a struggle. So I did what anyone would do in my situation and I looked his dad up in the white pages. I know, ballsy. But guess who got a hit! I called up the one Troy Ellis who would have been at a familiar street address. BINGO! Devale's mom answered the phone and to my surprise, she remembered exactly who I was, and we talked for a few. I wrapped the convo by telling her that I was going to Hofstra for a charity event and wanted to hit Devale up, so she gave me his phone number. I called him up and thought, "Let's just have a conversation and see how it goes."

My mom and dad had me under, as we say in the Caribbean, heavy manners. They weren't with me having a boyfriend, entertaining boys, or anything of the sort. That was not a conversation that we had in my house. But I wanted this college opportunity to be able to meet people, talk to guys, see what was out there, and have some fun. I remember getting ready to go to the Light the Night Walk and trying on a thousand outfits. I was like one of those girls that you see in a romantic movie where I'm going through all my clothes and practicing over and over again what I wanted to say to Devale when we finally met up. If I'm honest, there was also a part of me that was like, "Girl, why are you even getting all bent out of shape for this dude?" But I could feel that there was something intriguing about him and I knew that I had to go see what it was for myself. To my surprise, when I called Devale after what was now at least a month or two of his failed attempts to reach me, he recognized my voice and knew exactly who it was. I told him about the walk, and we agreed to meet up after the event wrapped and his study-hall hours. I had no idea what ride I was about to take with this familiar stranger.

Devale

During our first date at Hofstra, she came to see me after the Light the Night Walk. I just had to show off this pretty girl with the long hair and full lips to all my friends. Plus she had on these khaki pants that showed off every curve she was hiding under that gown I first saw her in. I took her to the student center and told her that she could get whatever she wanted at the cafeteria. I was thinking, "Let me splurge on shorty and show her what I'm working with." My boys were all waiting at the table to see this girl I'd been talking about all day. Sherief, Bo, Terry, and Pitt were all waiting to give me their thoughts. I introduced Kay to all of them. They were perfect gentlemen in that moment, but the minute she turned to get her phone I was bombarded with high fives and choreographed gyrating movements that signaled she passed the eye test. I urged them to stop for fear of getting caught and messing up my chances, but on the inside I was just as excited.

We got our food, walked back to my room, and I kid you not, it was almost as if I was speaking to a friend that I had known my entire life. We had only talked like this the day we first met at the banquet. She sat on my bed, took her shoes off, and then started devouring this turkey sandwich I bought her. She was eating it like she hadn't eaten in days. Mayonnaise on the corner of her mouth, pickle juice running down her chin, and crumbs from the chips she was inhaling were falling on the floor. She was so apologetic, and I was looking in awe at this little prissy beauty queen, thinking it was refreshing to see her sit on my bed and be so comfortable.

As we started our conversation, it led to us talking about our dreams and about what we wanted to do after college. I pointed to the TV screen and *Martin* just so happened to be on at the time, and I said, "I want to do that. I want to act." Khadeen didn't twist up her face or laugh at me like most people did at the time. She said, "That's what's up. So how you going to do that?" We talked about a plan of what I wanted to do. Then she told me she wanted to be in entertainment news, and we talked through her dreams and goals. It was the most organic, authentic conversation I had ever had in my life at that point. All the signs were saying, "Y'all are probably going to have sex tonight!" but sex never crossed our minds. We just talked and talked for hours. After we talked, we sat next to each other on my bed and she lay on my chest. It felt like we had been best friends forever.

One huge lesson that carried over from our early dating days into our marriage is to understand that everyone is not going to be on the same page at the same time. When we first started dating, I wasn't looking to be a boyfriend—and she was equally honest with me at the time that she wasn't looking to be anyone's girlfriend. But just two weeks later after we started dating, Khadeen told me she loved me. What am I supposed to do with that? All I did was say "Thank you." Fortunately, it didn't run Khadeen off, but it also showed Khadeen that I wasn't ready for that step right then, and she was able to receive that. That moment showed me that things can change quickly in a relationship and that Khadeen was ready for more than I was. But I didn't allow that to chase me off.

What it allowed me to learn in that moment, which carried into marriage, is that a good relationship is like a dance. It's a give-and-take. Sometimes you have to take a step back and think outside of yourself. Khadeen and I talk all the time about being of service in your marriage and understanding that that service is the most selfless act you can give someone when you are committed to dedicating your life to that someone. Khadeen and I understood early in our relationship that we weren't always on the same page, but I wanted to be of service to her as a friend, not just as a boyfriend. Having that mindset allowed us to grow.

You have to allow grace because grace is the only way you can think about what your partner may need in that moment, as opposed to what you need all the time. Now, as a married couple, wanting to be of service to my spouse and her wanting to be of service to me is something that has carried us from the time we first started dating.

Khadeen

The anxiousness and nerves had a magical way of disappearing once we were finally alone in each other's presence. I was shocked in that moment when I realized how calm I felt. We went back to his dorm room and nothing about it felt creepy or awkward at all. He never once made me feel uncomfortable. I was also fascinated by on-campus life because at the time, I was still commuting to and from school. I also had a feeling that Hofstra would be the college that I would ultimately transfer to. Devale may or may not have sealed the deal.

When I sat on Devale's bed, we spoke for almost four hours. It was the most natural, free-flowing conversation with no awkward pauses, no moments of trying to fill in the gaps with something funny or clever to say. Everything was just so effortless and comfortable. I was also taken aback by the level of affinity we had for each other right off the bat. Literally in that moment, I felt myself falling for Devale. At first, I wanted to fight it because I was like, "Girl, you didn't come here for this. You might potentially be in Boston or Maryland. And even if you end up at Hofstra, who said you want to even be with one person?" But, so as not to overthink things, I just succumbed to the feeling and rode the wave.

Devale has always been the perfect gentleman, and even in our moments together in his dorm room, he maintained the right amount of respectfulness that I was seeking. The walk back to my 1999 hunter green Toyota RAV4 felt like the longest walk ever. I think that's because I was playing in my mind how the night would end, which was already a picture perfect evening of pure vibes. When we got to the driver's side door, he opened it for me, and as my right leg stepped into the car, he pulled me back out toward him and we both leaned in for a kiss. And boy, did we kiss! His gentleness, yet undeniable passion, and my leaning and falling into this fairytale embrace was enough to make me want to stay in that utopia for hours.

When we had our first kiss, I didn't want to leave. There were immense butterflies in my stomach, and I kept thinking, "Oh my God, I can't believe this is happening." During my forty-minute car ride back to Brooklyn, I remember calling my cousin. She and I are like sisters, and she'd been waiting to hear from me about how the whole night went. As soon as she picked up, I said, "Girl, I might have met my husband tonight." And she said, "What? Your husband?"

"It was amazing," I said. "Everything was just so comfortable. I feel like I bumped into one of my old friends that I hadn't seen in years, and we were just catching up." I knew she was happy for me, but she still said, "All right, girl, I see you out here, but don't get too serious too fast. You got to keep your options open."

I remember going home that night and just beaming. Devale called me when I got in, and still to this day it's one of his pet peeves if I go somewhere and don't call him immediately to reassure that I'm okay and arrived safely. We made plans to see each other again, and we have spoken every single day since October 3, 2002.

So now you understand why I always tell my friends that it's okay for a woman to shoot her shot without worrying about if she appears too forward. I'll be honest—this wasn't as much of an issue when I was dating Devale in the early 2000s, before social media. I don't envy the dating community now because there's so much to unpack when you're looking to just be in that dating circle.

In that moment of approaching Devale first, that was one of my first opportunities to show myself that I could go after something I wanted in real time. From there, I had more courage to ultimately choose Hofstra as the school I transferred to and to begin to get to know myself and my dreams more authentically. The decision was also made for me when I received the most scholarship money from them versus the University of Maryland and Boston University. Happenstance or fate? Call it what you want but I believe this love was ordained far before we had any wind of each other. Choosing to honor how I felt in that moment, without worrying about what I should or shouldn't do, led to everything else that's happened since.

KHADEEN'S HOT TAKE

A Hero, a Pickle, and a Bag of Chips

When Devale and I were first dating, I'm grateful that we had this time of innocence where the simple things were enough for us. I can't imagine dating now in the age of social media. From the outside looking in, it looks like so many people have to filter who they are, and as a result they show up to their relationships as a representative of who they are because they are fearful of being ridiculed or judged. Or maybe the pressures of social media continually rob individuals of really connecting with their true self.

Devale didn't court me with expensive gifts or trips—he pulled me in with a hero sandwich, a bag of chips, and a pickle on the side. He connected with me through honest, meaningful conversation—and, of course, his wit and charisma. Those simple times that we spent together in the beginning felt so right because we weren't comparing ourselves to anybody else. When we let ourselves simply be comfortable with what felt good to us, our love escalated quickly and there was no denying how we genuinely felt. The hours that Devale and I spent together in college just hanging out in each other's dorm rooms or taking cheap trips up and down the East Coast gave us *hours* of quality time that built the foundation for our marriage.

The courting process should be about building trust and showing the other person that you care. It shouldn't be a competition with anyone else to vacation somewhere exotic like Bali or Bora Bora or to pressure your man into getting you a ring outside of his budget. If happiness for you is taking a simple weekend break to Virginia Beach and having a small courthouse wedding with the folks you love—do that. Don't spend your energy trying to live up to someone else's Instagram posts. Bring your real self to the table and court that special someone on the level where you are comfortable.

For now, be good with that person who can get you that hero, pickle, and bag of chips. If they are worth going the distance with, there will be plenty of time to upgrade your dating game, and ultimately your marriage game, in the future.

Chapter Two

Stuck Between
Your Love and a Hard Place

A strong love doesn't just help you get through the good times, but the rough times as well. If you want to see what your relationship is really made of, you have to be willing to get into the trenches and learn how to get through the hard places together. Petty arguments about missing a birthday or leaving a toilet seat up become really minor when you have to face the reality of losing a loved one, being downsized from a job or losing a business, and slamming up against an unexpected financial emergency.

After twenty years of living and loving our way through terminating our first pregnancy (we'll get to that part later in the book), reconfiguring our lives after the NFL, and trying to rebuild our financial future when the entire country was in a financial free fall, we know a thing or two about loving our way through the hard times. We discovered that when you are in the middle of a crisis, love has to go from being a noun to a verb. Sometimes this kind of love will look like putting the other person's comfort before your own. Other times love means that you have to choose yourself before you can be of service to your partner. Love should never look like abuse or unending sacrifice, but you have to know what you are willing to do to allow your love to surpass your present reality and get you moving toward your shared goals and purpose.

What does it mean to get unstuck from your hard places? What does it look like when you have to carry more of the load in your relationship for a period of time? How do you know if this is just a bump in the road or if it's a permanent barricade in your relationship? It's something that every couple has to find out for themselves. But it's worth asking yourself the question: Does my partner show up for me in the ways that I need them to?

We had to learn early on what it means to be in love and to navigate the very real realities of some of our hardest places.

Devale

Growing up in a Southern Baptist household with both my parents and a lot of rules, my mom and dad did not talk to me or my siblings about sex ever. The only conversation I had with my father about sex was when I was sixteen and he simply said, "You know I got condoms in my drawer, right?"

In my Christian family, the only conversation I really had was about abstinence, abstinence, and more abstinence. Everybody knows teenagers have sex, but they act like it never happens.

So being on campus by myself, with my own room and a woman that I was falling in love with, was the first feeling of liberation I've ever had in my life. At eighteen years old, I felt like I had my life figured out. My grades were good. I was doing well on the football team. I had this beautiful girl that I could see every single day. I felt like I was winning and that I had accomplished something in my life.

For the first time, I felt like a full adult, and Khadeen and I felt like we were on top of the world. There wasn't a day that went by where we weren't exploring each other's bodies and on top of each other multiple times a day. When I first got to Hofstra, Khadeen was still at Brooklyn College. She used to come up and see me about twice a week—and whenever she showed up, it was on and popping!

One day, we were making out and kissing with Khadeen on top of me. All of a sudden, I felt her just pull her panties to the side and go to work. I thought, "Wow, this is really happening right now! You better not cum too fast." And I didn't. Y'all know things like that matter to an eighteen-year-old young man. I felt good about the way it happened, mainly because I represented well for the homies (smile if you know what I'm talking about), and also because I didn't push it on her or make her feel uncomfortable. I have to admit that we were a little bit reckless because we didn't use a condom. Okay, we were a lot bit reckless, but we were feeling each other in the moment, and it was freaking amazing.

Khadeen

If I could bottle up that sweet spot in college when I was nine-teen years old, I would happily take a swig of that every now and again. Devale and I were just intoxicated with living in that moment of being in love and experiencing all the emo-tions at the maximum high. It felt good to just be free and in love because we had the space, the opportunity, and the time to do so.

It was in Devale's bosom that I earned my first and only C ever. I will never forget this dreadful math class. I was not a huge fan of mathematics but I did what I had to do to get by. As long as I was able to count my coins, I was A-okay. And getting by for me was earning at minimum a B/B+, no mat-ter the subject. That was the standard in my household grow-ing up—90 percent or better. I remember being so annoyed when I would come home elated with a 94 percent on an exam, only to be asked "Where are the other six points?" I guess that was my parents' way of encouraging me to learn from my mistakes and aim higher. Noted, but damn. But not in this class. The professor was a drag, and I'm not sure who told my ass to take an 8 am to 9:35 am class on Tuesdays and Thursdays during the spring semester, because snuggling with Devale on those cold-ass winter into spring mornings was worth risking it all and missing every class.

This little world that I shared with Devale was just full of so much love, passion, and friendship that it was really easy for us to be careless, too. When you're young and in love, there's a bit of invincibility that you possess. I started thinking, "We're just so in love and we have the freedom to do whatever we want. Whatever the consequences, we'll get through it together." So that was a great time for us. I was away from my parents' house and I finally felt like the adult I was itching to be. I now had the freedom to do what I wanted to do and there was nobody to tell me otherwise.

Everybody was hooking up on campus, so I felt comfort in knowing that I was doing it with only Devale. Once I arrived on campus at Hofstra, it was pretty much known that I was Devale's girl, and when anybody saw him, he was known as Khadeen's man. Nobody tried to infiltrate our relationship too much, which was good.

With neither of us being sexually well versed prior to meeting each other, it was really an opportunity for us to get to know what we liked and what we didn't like. Much like Devale, I came from a background where talk about anything related to sex was not discussed at all by my father, and if my mom dared to even broach the subject, there was always an awkwardness when it came to those kinds of conversations.

My mom and I bonded over my pageant experiences. She was always my biggest fan and supporter when it came to pageant preparations, fittings, coaching classes, rehearsals, community service work, and so much more. My mother legitimately stopped at nothing to empower me to take on anything I showed interest in. She made sure I was prepared, had the best of the best, and always hit the stage looking and feeling confident. I looked forward to our mini girls' weekend getaways.

I remember the first time I told my mother that I was having sex. It was such an awkward conversation. We were traveling to see the Miss America pageant in Atlantic City. She and I drove to New Jersey to link up with a couple of other pageant friends. At this time, Devale and I had been dating for at least two years. I was thinking she just has to already know or assume that I was having sex. I'd been dating the same guy for two years—what exactly did she think was going to happen? Especially being away from home on campus. But knowing my mom and the way she lives in this world of denial at times, I should have known that she would've been taken aback when I finally confirmed to her that we were indeed having sex. Perhaps she assumed that Devale and I weren't as serious, because during this time Devale was turned off by my mom's disdain for him and our relationship and it forced him to keep his distance. And to keep peace, I didn't talk about him much at home. I wanted to protect my "happy place" at all costs.

The conversation came up awkwardly while we were having dinner over the course of that weekend. When I told her that I was actively having sex, she almost choked on the steak she was eating at the time. I remember her saying, "I expected that you were going to wait until marriage." I said, "I'm sorry you feel that way. And to be quite honest, you were five months pregnant with me when you got married. So you didn't wait until marriage, either. I don't know what made you think I was just going to miraculously wait until marriage." I don't know what gave me the courage to say that to my mom, but at the time I knew that I was in love with Devale and I felt good that I wasn't out there having sex with a bunch of guys. I had to be okay with disappointing her and learning how to grow into the woman I wanted to be, walking in my truth all while loving the man I was with.

I've always had a healthy fear of my mom and concurrently a burdening fear of disappointing her and my dad. My parents worked hard and bearing witness to this alone was enough for me to want to be a stellar daughter and good human being. As the firstborn for my parents and first grandchild and niece on the maternal side, there was a lot of pressure on me to be the prime example. I was setting a standard for my siblings and cousins whether or not I agreed to this task. I never liked feeling like I couldn't be candid with my family or open about the way I felt. And this is not so much because I tried and failed, but instead, I was never encouraged to do so. That may be in part why my relationship with Devale was so free flowing and encapsulating. For once in my life, I felt seen, heard, and was motivated to speaking my truth on a level I never experienced at home. Shit, I did not know how to eloquently articulate my feelings or thoughts some-times. Expression of self within a Caribbean household has historically been met with vitriol or taken as disrespect no matter how tactful the approach. I had to learn with Devale how to develop my thoughts and emotions internally first, and then how to effectively express them without fear of ridicule, shame, or heightened emotion. In retrospect, Devale and I were having therapy sessions throughout college, working on ourselves as a collective and aiding each other as individuals.

When I think about it now, I had nerve popping that hot shit to my mom. She really could have let me have it right then and there. Maybe a part of her appreciated my trans-parency. Maybe a part of her was too disappointed to admit it. Either way, it was a freeing feeling to be able to finally speak from a place of truth with her.

Devale and I were naturally building levels of intimacy from the minute that we had our first kiss. That was enough to make me more intrigued and want to be around him more, and of course, in due time, in a more intimate manner. Each time I visited his dorm room, our make-out sessions progres-sively got more touchy-feely. I was building up this time frame in my mind of when I wanted to have sex with him.

My favorite cousin told me, "Girl, we have to let these boys wait at least three months, and then after that you can let it rip." With Devale, it was a fight for me because I was very attracted to him *and* I wanted to be able to demand this level of respect from this man simultaneously. I wanted to let him know that I was in this for the long haul. I didn't want to be somebody you could smash and run because I genuinely felt that I had more to offer and I truly valued the bond we were building. Devale and I had our first date in October, so I thought to myself, "Okay, Khadeen, you can hold out until Valentine's Day. That will be a perfect time to have sex with him for the first time."

But that date went out the window after one too many make-out sessions. Devale and I had sex for the first time a month later in early November and I was actually the one to make the first move as Devale was being the perfect gentleman.

Once again, here I was taking the lead, and I'm thinking to myself, "Khadeen, who are you, girl? First you approached him, and now you're taking the lead on sex? What's going on with you?" When I think back to it now, I can only shake my head at the level of carelessness in that intimate moment. But, in truth, being so consumed with young love at the moment, it just happened, and it was great. It was everything. It was one of our most memorable moments. We had sex very regularly after that. The intrigue and coincidence that started this relationship were merely seedlings that blossomed into a relationship rooted in a deep love and soul connection. And the sex, definitely an added bonus.

Devale

By the spring of 2004, Khadeen and I knew we were playing Russian roulette. Every month after we started having unprotected sex, we were trying to clock her period. But I knew that Khadeen and I were just being reckless, irresponsible kids by thinking we could do all our research on WebMD. Between Google and all the old wives' tales I learned from listening to teammates and "older cousins" I really wasn't related to, I thought I had everything under control. We had been gambling like this for a matter of months now, and since we were successful, I just knew I was the master of the pull-out game. One day she told me that she didn't feel any of her normal PMS symptoms and after three days I nervously said, "You think you want to take a pregnancy test?" Khadeen got a pregnancy test and went into the bathroom. In my heart, I knew what was gonna happen when she walked out the door with that test, but I was still in denial. I said to myself, ". . . She ain't pregnant! If you keep thinking she's pregnant, then she's gonna be pregnant! So just stop thinking she's pregnant and *know* that she's not pregnant." When Kay stepped out of that bathroom the news was written all over her face: She was pregnant.

Khadeen

As Devale and I were deep in doing grown folks things, it's only natural that grown folks situations and consequences forced me to put on my big-girl panties. When I found out that I was pregnant, that feeling of invincibility that Devale and I had around us immediately shattered. Getting pregnant at nineteen really threw both of us for a loop. Initially, I was happy about the idea of knowing that it was possible that I could conceive a child and that I could do it with someone who I loved so much. I was in a mental tug-of-war, thinking there was no way I could have a baby now one minute and in the next, I was daydreaming about what our baby would look like.

But it didn't take a hot second for reality to set in and I started to panic when I thought about what I would tell my parents. There was instant disappointment in myself and an instant fear of disappointing my family. I also felt some loneliness because I knew that I wouldn't have much support from any other women in my family outside of my favorite cousin. I was too bogged down by fear and I just knew I had to handle this without help or advice from anyone.

I am a girl who has the regular twenty-eight-day cycles. If my cycle reaches day 29 or 30, I knew there would be a reason to be suspicious. When I found out that I was pregnant and I told Devale, I remember instantly feeling so many emotions at one time. I remember crying, falling into his arms, and just lying in bed. When Devale was questioning me about how I felt and what I wanted to do, I was taken aback. But this was good because I knew that I really had a partner in whatever I decided to do.

After breaking the news to him, I kept looking over at the still saturated First Response test—the one where you can get the results five days earlier. It's as if I expected it to change to a negative. Instead, that undeniable crimson line appeared as if it was getting darker and deeper, as my eyes welled with tears. I struggled so much with feeling like I was just going to be another college-age statistic, whether or not I kept this pregnancy. I battled with doing what I felt was right, what would optically look "good" to others, and tried to consider what Devale would want.

Devale

At that moment, I felt stuck because I don't think that it's a man's responsibility to tell a woman what she should do with her body. I knew that, ultimately, she was going to be the one who would have to make all the changes to bring a new life into this world. All that I could say in that moment was "I support whatever decision you make."

But then Khadeen asked me again, "Well, what do you think?" I said, "I know that I love you and if you want to, we can find a way to make it work because my family's super supportive. I feel like your family would be supportive, too, if this was what we had to do. But if you feel like this is something you really don't want to do, I'll rock with you on that, too." The truth of the matter is I'm a "glass is half full" type of guy. On top of that, I always feel like I'm capable of finding a way to always put more into the glass. That hasn't always worked out in my favor, but it's the only way I know how to operate. Kay, on the other hand, is more of a "This whole glass is fucking broken" type of chick. And she has never had any problems letting me know that my optimism is not her reality.

It didn't take long for Khadeen to say, "No, Devale, I don't want to do this. I don't want to be someone's baby mama and have to possibly drop out of school and possibly put the things that I want to do for myself on hold." While I understood her decision, I'm not going to lie, it hurt. I felt like this life was a blessing and we shouldn't get to decide when it is or is not time for a life to come from us. But out of love for Khadeen and what we were trying to build, I was in full support of her making the decision to not have this child. For the first time I can recall in my life, someone else had emptied my glass. And I say that loosely because it was also Kay's glass. For the first time ever, I had to look at the glass with a different perspective.

Khadeen

I come from a household where communication and discussions about feelings were not really stimulated or encouraged. It was never for lack of love. Love was in abundance in my house and that was evident and felt. I did, however, witness very little healthy communication between my parents, which in turn caused a lot of grief and strife within their own relationship. As a child, I always held my position, and out of respect, I stayed in my place and never intervened. Devale grew up in a very opposite environment where conversation among them was paramount. If there was a disagreement, his mom called a family caucus like you used to see on *The Cosby Show*. Coming from two completely different lines and methods of communication was very different for me. I was used to not knowing how to effectively express myself and Devale was used to overexpressing himself. In our early days, he really had to pull my feelings out of me and push me to share how I felt. I was poor at making decisions and very indecisive. In the beginning, I met Devale's overeager approach to talk, discuss, and share with a lot of silence because I just didn't know how to express myself candidly or transparently.

So telling my parents about this pregnancy was never an option. Like ever. Fortunately, when I decided not to move forward with this pregnancy, I was glad that I was in a very safe place with Devale and that we could make this decision together. I felt that regardless of the decision I made, he was going to be there by my side 110 percent (ladies, take note!). I was leaning more in the direction of terminating the pregnancy because I didn't feel like keeping the baby was an option at the time based on where we were in our lives, the things that we wanted to do, and the potential scrutiny from our families and our peers. It wasn't an easy decision, but we felt like in that moment it was just best for us. We also knew that we wanted to provide a certain kind of life for our potential children, and we knew that we just weren't equipped to do that in that moment.

After I was firm in my decision, I googled and did my research on some of the better places in the area to go ahead with the termination. I wanted to go somewhere that was a little bit more private and with an office that could really take care of me. Fortunately, I made the right choice because leading up to that day, I had a lot of support from the center that I ultimately chose.

I called the clinic about five times and hung up before finally allowing the phone to ring. Upon answering, I struggled to even get the words out. "I would like to . . . I think I want to schedule . . . I'm pregnant and would like more information about . . . termination." Abortion, terminate, pregnant—all words that haunted me in that moment because I just always thought it would never be me. But here I was, counting back to the first day of my last period and getting the rundown on what to expect on my appointment day. I hung up and sobbed. Now, I was terrified about this upcoming procedure, convinced that God would never bless me with any children ever again and petrified that someone, mainly my parents, would find out. Through all this, Devale was present, compassionate, and concerned. Any trace of worry or doubt dissipated in his presence.

But even in feeling confident in my decision, there was still an eerie feeling that I felt nonstop as the days led up to the appointment. I remember Devale being so insanely attentive and supportive, and whenever I called him, he was willing to drop everything in that moment. I know he had gotten permission from one of his coaches to be there for me, which was great. Devale's coach was the one adult who knew what was going on, and the fact that he was just so supportive of Devale made me feel a lot better about the situation. I also told my favorite cousin, and she was willing to support me however she could, which I appreciated. But Devale's coach and my cousin were literally the only two people who knew what was happening. At that time, honestly, all I felt like I needed was Devale. As long as he was by my side, I could pretty much do anything. For the first time, we were doing something together as a team, under incredibly emotionally tough circumstances.

Devale

Before the day of the procedure, I checked in with my receiver coach on the football team. As a young athlete, you always had to speak with your position coach about anything off the field that was happening with you. I knew that I was going to have to be the one to take Khadeen to do the procedure and also make sure that she was taken care of during that process.

I pulled my coach aside and I told him that Khadeen was pregnant. Khadeen and I had become a big deal on campus.

People knew who we were, and my coach knew Khadeen because she used to come and scream for us at all the games and practices. The first thing he asked me was "Is she okay?" I told him that everything was okay and that she had planned on terminating the pregnancy.

Just as I was about to ask him for some time to be with her, my coach said to me, "Let me explain something to you, young man. You are not to come back to practice until that young lady is perfectly fine." All I could say was "Yes, sir." He dismissed me from practice early and I went back home to Khadeen. I had to put on a confident front to be a support system for Kay. I knew her heart was filled with the same conviction as mine, but she was literally carrying all the burden. If there was ever a time to be selfless and of service to someone else, it was in this moment.

Taking On the Hard Things—Together

Khadeen

I was sleepless the night before the appointment and I remember waking up to a dreary and gloomy day. I found a place that was about fifteen minutes away from our college. Whenever I go back home to Long Island and I drive past exit 33 on the Long Island Expressway, I'm immediately taken back to the day of that appointment.

I was so glad that I chose a place where they didn't treat me like a number. They treated me like a person. I had some fears that I would be faced with scrutiny or judgment and I would hear someone say something like "Oh God, here's another young girl coming in here to have an abortion because she was being careless." But when I got there, I felt really super comfortable and supported.

When I made the appointment, the receptionist told me that they only did termination procedures on specific days. So when I glanced to my left and then to my right, I saw women of various ages and ethnicities who were all presumably in the same boat as me. The waiting room was silent; News 12 Long Island played on the television but with closed captions and no sound. Nonetheless, the silence in there was a palpable feeling of support and camaraderie. My empty stomach was growling, going on ten hours of no food or liquids.

Once they took my blood work and I changed into a gown, I was led to a very sterile and cold table. There's nothing cozy about these offices. The doctor and I had a concise, straightforward convo explaining how the procedure would work, how long it would be, and what I should expect. Or at least I think he discussed this because in that moment, I was in a daze of praying, debating if I would really go through with this, and talking myself into staying calm. The anesthesiologist gave me his spiel and there was no turning back. I left my shoulda, coulda, woulda right there, too. But I do remember the nurse being by my side and just listening to all the sounds. After that, the doctor came in, did an ultrasound, and then put me under.

Devale

When we finally pulled up to the office, I wasn't allowed to go inside. She had to go inside and do all the paperwork by herself, but I sat outside the entire time. I remember giving her a big hug and kiss before she went inside. I told her that I wasn't going to leave until the appointment was over.

As I sat out there in the car, I started to cry. I was just afraid that something was going to happen to her. I did not want to be the person to have to go to her parents and say, "Something happened to Khadeen, and it was my fault." I was just super anxious. I also cried because I felt like she and I were just being irresponsible. I felt like we weren't thinking about ourselves. We weren't thinking about all the values and morals that our parents had raised us with. I felt like I was letting my parents down. I felt like I let Khadeen's parents down.

Khadeen

When I woke up, I was wheeled into a recovery room. I was crying and begging God for forgiveness nonstop. I felt like this was probably going to be something that I would be punished for later. I was struck with the guilt of terminating such a precious gift and also mad at myself for being so negligent altogether. I didn't think I would get that emotional. I remember just telling God that the next time a child chooses me, I'm not going to take it for granted. Just then the nurse came back into the room and said, "It's okay. You're okay. Everything is done and you're going to be fine." All I could blurt out was "I swear I'm a good person and my boyfriend is a good person, too." Before I could get another word out, the nurse said, "You don't have to explain yourself to me. All you have to focus on is getting better now. I promise you that you'll be fine." Whenever I think of that nurse, I'm always grateful that she was so reassuring and kind to me.

The best moment of that tough day was seeing Devale when he came to pick me up. We both cried again, but there was now relief that I had made it out of the procedure alive and well. I just wanted to go back to my dorm room, sleep, and recover from it. I wanted to pretend like it never happened and resume normalcy in my life, but nothing would ever be the same after that.

Devale

As Khadeen limped to the car, I helped her get inside. I asked her how she was feeling, and she quietly said, "Fine, but I just want to go lie down." As I watched the tears roll down her face, I felt for her in the moment and I breathed a sigh of relief knowing that she was okay. I was dedicated to making sure that she would be okay from here on out.

The biggest thing that I've learned from that experience is that for the first time I felt like I had a partner. She literally became the Bonnie to my Clyde. She was just as concerned about me every step of the way as I was for her. I knew after the procedure that I was going to sit by her side every minute and only go to class. A few days afterward, I remember lying with Khadeen and she said to me, "Hey, don't you got practice?" I told her that my coach told me that I had permission to stay with her until she got back to normal.

She immediately said, "No, Devale. Go to practice. This is spring ball and I don't want you to miss out on your chance to play." This was a total shocker to me because here we are just days after making this huge decision that could have had an adverse outcome to her health and she was thinking ahead to my future. This was the opposite of everything I had ever thought I would hear from a woman in a moment like this. What came out of that super dark cloud was realizing that I had a partner for life.

At first, Khadeen's decision to terminate our first pregnancy hurt me because growing up in a Christian home, you hear about how wrong abortions are and that it's considered murder. But I had to understand that creating a life comes with a huge amount of sacrifice and risk to the woman. If she decides on her own terms that this is something she doesn't want to do, that's something I would have to learn to live with as a man, because I knew that I couldn't tell her what to do with her body.

Most people have issues in their relationship after a loss of a child or an abortion because of communication. People typically spend most of their time arguing about how they communicate as opposed to dealing with the issue that is at hand. When Khadeen and I went through the experience of terminating our first pregnancy, I learned that we communicate extremely well. We are super honest about what we want and what we need, but we're also very empathetic towards each other. I believe that's important in a relationship because when you know that your partner not only tells you that they understand, but they also make the effort to feel what you're feeling, it makes the choice to be with someone that much easier. For a lot of men, typically when you get a young lady pregnant, you hear all these stories about the guy who just wants her to have an abortion because he doesn't want to have a baby. There are also stories of men who are in relationships with women they love and the timing may not be right, and it's okay for you as a man to feel like, "I love this person, but I'm not ready to have a child with her yet."

For any man reading this and facing the realness of terminating a pregnancy, I would encourage you to think outside of yourself for a minute and consider what might be going through the heart and mind of the woman who is carrying the child before you try to make a decision for her. Parenthood is not easy, and based on what I know now with four sons of my own, I would have made a better decision about how Khadeen and I got into being intimate at a younger age. I definitely would've used protection. I would've found a way for her and me to have sex in a fun way without putting her at risk. If I could do it all over again, I would change how reckless Khadeen and I had been due to being young, free, and in love at that time.

Khadeen

Through that situation, I believe that Devale and I transformed into adults. I learned so much about the power of leaning into each other. This experience taught us how to be responsible, hold ourselves accountable moving forward, and work together as a team. We got through this moment of adversity and it made us that much closer. I was also further comforted in a moment when Devale held my face, looked deeply into my eyes, and told me that he wanted nothing more than for me to be the mother of his children, but, we both knew, just not now.

After that experience and still to this day, I love and appreciate Devale for relentlessly taking the time to understand where I'm coming from so that we could both move forward accordingly. I've come to realize that in his diligence and determination to understand me, the communication that I wasn't used to turned out to be so productive for us. We were able to be more proactive than reactive when it came to dealing with each other because we both sought a level of trust and clarity. Sometimes we do agree to disagree, but the level of understanding that he and I take away from every conversation, every discussion, every debate that we have is what helps us to grow our level of respect for each other. It absolves us of any misunderstanding or misconstruing of what is happening between us and our family.

We are fully invested in understanding where the other person is coming from. Even though we may not agree about everything, we each have the ability and willingness to understand how each other feels. It truly took a lot of work for us to be able to be that transparent and candid with each other at such a young age as we chose to end our first pregnancy. Every day since then, I'm proud of how we've tackled every hardship that has come our way.

Chapter Three

Creating a New Kind of Love Story

We both grew up in homes where so much was left unsaid. Both sets of parents were more concerned with keeping up appearances than they were with taking on the problems at hand and setting a good example for us and our siblings. It was frustrating for us to grow up in homes where there would be weeks and sometimes months of simmering tensions without resolution.

Learning how to manage conflicts in a marriage or a relationship is not for the faint of heart. Discovering our individual communication styles was incredibly hard as we started our relationship. Devale was more used to handling breakdowns straight on and Khadeen was conflict avoidant. It wasn't uncommon for us to bump heads about how to resolve something as small as deciding where we wanted to go for dinner when we were dating to something as big as choosing our priorities after our wedding. We were determined that when we created our own family we would make a new narrative for our sons. We didn't want our children to go through the challenges of not being able to express their feelings or sitting in shame because of a mistake. We were focused on creating an open home where our sons didn't have to worry about whether it was okay to be their authentic selves.

Maybe you've been dealing with the challenges of breaking old family patterns and dealing with generational trauma. It's not an easy task. But the benefits of starting new, healthy traditions far outweigh the difficulties in terms of building a stronger family unit. Hopefully, our experiences will help you realize something about your own ingrained behaviors or the relationship models you had growing up.

Khadeen

Devale and I never sought out to be #RelationshipGoals. In fact, we don't profess to be that at all. We just believe that there is power in sharing our experiences. We receive so many DMs, emails, messages, and letters from our podcast listeners who say things like "Thank you for saving my marriage," or "You helped me to spark this conversation with my husband or my wife because we're going through the same exact thing as the two of you."

Sometimes I worry that people will say "Oh my God, the Ellises share everything," or that they may get tired of us.

But, in truth, we're very strategic about what we share. We're intentional about sharing things that we think may benefit other couples, particularly other millennials who are also trying to break free of these generational cycles, curses, and traumas.

Early on in our relationship, I remembered Devale's mom saying, "Don't get into the habit of making his plates. His hands work." I was really caught off guard and I replied to her, "I actually don't mind making his plate." And I thought to myself, "Don't you want me to take care of your son?!" My mom also gave me similar advice and said, "Don't start making habits in your relationship that you can't keep." I know where both of them were coming from. They didn't want me to fall into old patterns about "serving your man first," and both of our moms were very adamant about expressing their concern about us being individuals first before we became wholeheartedly attached to another person. Devale stood up for me and said to his mom, "Don't impose in my relationship and tell my girlfriend not to do something that we both enjoy."

To be honest, I don't believe that his mom's or my mom's statements were coming from a place of malice. I think they each had their own life experiences that forced them to feel this way. This is in part why it can be problematic to take advice about relationships from others and apply it to your own relationship without dissecting the entire scope and context. Everyone naturally brings their own biases into scenarios. Maybe in that moment, for argument's sake, Devale's mom made that comment because she was privy to him being spoiled and was trying to break him from it long before I even came around. Or perhaps my mom had been burned in the past by not being able to or wanting to maintain habits she started because they weren't received well or reciprocated. I've learned to take what I want from advice, solicited or unsolicited, and leave the rest. Most times, those in your corner are there because ultimately you trust their judgment or presence in your life. Others you know are around simply for vibes and you'd never take their opinion, even on the latest limited Lay's chips flavor. Moral of the story, a hit dog will holler—even when you didn't ask. And I mean, who said you even like dogs to begin with?!

When I was growing up, my grandmother would make dinner for the family. Before anyone could touch the meal, she took out my grandfather's portion and set it aside in his little Pyrex dish. His portion was not to be touched because his dinner had to be on the table, warmed up, and ready for him when he got home from work. Everyone else ate after he did and his plate had to be made first. That's what I saw growing up from my grandmother and then from my mom for a short period of time. But having seen that, I also just wanted my husband (or boyfriend at the time) to feel like he was being taken care of. That was a love language of mine to him. It was one of those things where you take the advice with a grain of salt, and if you need to throw it in the pot, do that. If not, let it rock.

Devale

I'm thankful that our families did not get involved in our marriage. It allowed us to work things out on our own terms. Making our own decisions allowed us to find our own process because we discovered that one process doesn't fit all. If you try to listen to other people and say "I'm going to handle this situation the way he or she did," you are more than likely going to fail by trying to follow someone else's template for love. When you fail at someone else's rule book, you can have a tendency to believe you are not equipped for marriage, and that's probably not true. You just have to find the rule book that works for *you*.

Through trial and error, Khadeen and I have found what works for us—and the funny thing is, we're still finding it out. After being together for more than twenty years now, we still have conversations about changes that are happening within each of us. But now we know how to deal with them differently because we don't rely on anyone else to give us advice. When I'm seeking answers within my marriage, I look within my marriage—and most important, I look to my spouse.

You will never become the best version of yourself by trying to emulate someone else. They have already mastered being them, and any attempt to be more perfect than them will always leave you feeling inadequate. Same goes for your relationship. No one can be more perfect than you at being you. Kay and I have learned over time that peace within our relationship starts with the absence of comparison. The thing that makes each relationship exceptional can only be found in its uniqueness.

It's like a diamond, right? A diamond is made with immense amounts of pressure in the dark, just like a marriage. When nobody else is watching, and you're in the dark, and it's just you two and all this pressure to try to be perfect: the ideal couple with the ideal marriage. That's when diamonds are created, when you two can figure out in that dark space, and with all this pressure, how to shine. Embracing what others may deem as flaws will only speak to a diamond's authenticity. The flaws tell the story. That is what creates a strong marriage.

Kay came from a family that didn't talk openly about issues, while I came from a family that held caucuses to discuss family shortcomings. She tended to shut down during conversations and get extremely quiet. I honestly felt like she was a spoiled little princess who was babied her whole life and often questioned our relationship's longevity if I couldn't be honest about the way I felt. I was used to being picked apart and learned to appreciate the criticism because it made me better. I became addicted to accountability because it was the only way I could defend my feelings. When I was in middle school, I started to hold my parents accountable for their words. When they said things, I remembered them verbatim as a way to prevent being piled on during the next family caucus. That became my greatest line of defense—being a stickler for details and learning how to use people's words against them in a debate. It was all about winning and never about understanding the other person's perspective. I had to win every argument with Kay early on to prove to her that she should value my opinion. It took years for me to figure out that that approach was doing more harm than good.

I would say that 95 percent of the relationships I grew up watching, and not just my parents, were couples bickering behind closed doors and then pretending that everything was perfect when they were in a public forum. I knew that I didn't want to live that kind of life with anyone, especially not my wife.

I believe that this is why it has been so important for me to be transparent with Khadeen. I knew that when I got married I wanted to be able to say freely "I love you" to my wife without having to wait for a special occasion. I remember one of my friends who got married before me told me that I would never love my wife as much as I loved her the moment I proposed. His advice to me was to understand that women prepare for the wedding while it's our responsibility as men to prepare for the marriage. Time and children will change everything. Less money, less time, and definitely less sex because of the latter. He said the best I could do was make as much money as I could to be able to provide a life my children would remember and enjoy because that was all that mattered once you got married. Do what you gotta do to keep your kids happy and your wife quiet. That conversation had me stressed the fuck out, but I took it with a grain of salt. Once again, I felt like my situation was different and I was willing to do whatever I had to do to not live like him and his wife. So I did the opposite. I chose transparency.

Khadeen

If there's one thing a West Indian parent is going to do, they're going to be concerned about how everything looks to other people, sometimes to the detriment of their own well-being. I was raised to not tell people my business and to be overly concerned with how things appear. Most of my life I heard "What will people think if——?" I never really understood this idea, but I just went with the flow of what I was taught. I was determined to be the obedient, goody-two-shoes child and not to ruffle any feathers. The truth is that I had so much love and respect for my parents that I was willing to do anything to make their job as parents easier.

Now that I've been with Devale for almost twenty years, I truly flipped and reversed those family patterns on their head. I'm coming to a point in my life where I don't even give a shit what people think or have to say. Releasing myself from the judgment of other people is the only reason why I'm able to exist in the public eye, particularly since Devale and I are so open on social media. I've witnessed early on that it doesn't matter what you do, people are always going to have something to say. Learning to break myself free of that has been so liberating. At the same time, it's been sad to see the lack of progress and happiness in some of my family members' lives because of the facade they are determined to keep putting out in the world. Whether it's a facade or fear, neither is a healthy option when you are seeking to exist as your authentic self. You really have to ask yourself, What does this person's opinion mean to me? How will this opinion affect me ultimately? Will I be happier if I decide to go against the grain?

There was always a completely polar-opposite dynamic between my parents. To this day, I still don't understand how the two of them ended up together. I know they say that opposites attract, but knowing my parents as I do now, theirs was truly an odd match. I feel like I can finally address them as an adult child and have the conversations I've always so desperately wanted to have. One thing I'm also careful to maintain is a listening ear, utmost respect, and no judgment because my parents are human and deserve grace.

I recently said to my mom, "What was it about Dad that made the two of you come together? From what I've seen over the years, y'all just don't match!"

My mom replied, "Your father was just a nice guy and I thought if he saw my ambition and saw me working hard toward certain things, that that would excite him, too." She said she thought that that was going to happen, and it never did. My father was content with coming up here from Saint Vincent and doing better than he was doing down there. My dad worked hard, sometimes at two jobs to provide. That was his sole purpose—to provide the basics that this family would need. My father loves in a way that isn't very affectionate or performative. His love is pure and basic, yet deep and understood.

I've had to learn to lean in to and be a receiver of my dad's way of loving. His love shows up boldly in how he sweetly cares for his grandsons—the after-school pickups, bonding over walks and ice cream truck rundowns, never missing a practice or game. It's randomly putting a little money in the boys' accounts or attending an open bar event only for him to say "Hey let me buy you a drink!" I may be able to count on one hand how many times my dad has verbally said "I love you" but I never questioned his love for me. To my surprise, he's becoming way more expressive now with me, my boys, and the family in general. To me, that's proof that how you love can be infectious and oftentimes reciprocated simply because your actions have made someone feel good. You may have tapped into an area in his or her life that has been starved or never been nourished. Or maybe grandchildren really do open a different side of folks because some days I barely recognize these softies who are grandparenting my boys now, but I love to see it and I love this for all of them.

My parents worked super hard over the years to pull money together to do real estate investments. At one point, they owned three properties in Brooklyn. This was huge for two teenagers who migrated from their respective countries to make something of themselves. They did make a lot of smart decisions early on in their marriage that we've greatly benefited from as children. There's a quote I read that stuck with me from an article featuring Lena Waithe: "No one should go to their grave with a dream deferred." I feel like neither of my parents lived out their full potential as individuals and as a unit because there was a disconnect in their relationship. They didn't have a partnership. Or it started out that way. But changed over the years. It's been heartbreaking to watch everything around them dissipate when it could have been so much better.

This is why I've always wanted my relationship with Devale to be much different than what I saw with my parents because I saw so much genuine unhappiness. In particular with my mom; she had to defer many of her dreams, hopes, and desires because she and my dad were so completely different. My mom was super ambitious, and she always wanted more out of life. Meanwhile my dad was satisfied with having a roof over his head and making sure that his family was fed and there was money in his bank account.

My mom is by far the hardest working person I know. I've never seen anyone so dedicated and committed to their career. Over the years, I learned that this commitment was mainly because she was working in overdrive to provide me and my siblings with the life she never had but always dreamed of. Migrating to America from Jamaica alone at the tender age of seventeen is where her story begins. Her parents sent her here to make something of herself and pursue her nursing dreams. She stayed with family friends, worked at Burger King while putting herself through school, and sent whatever she could back home to her younger siblings and parents. This was a common scenario for many West Indian families.

Sheron Joseph is my hero. She is the reason I was able to take chances as a child, try different interests, and become well rounded as a student. She believes in all that I am and will be. From academics, to dance, to pageants, my mom saw something in me early on that only a mom can see. For this, I'm so eternally grateful. As a child, I would witness her up in the wee hours of the mornings, writing notes, and completing paperwork for her job. With little to no sleep, she would be on the move again the next day. She was working as a home-care nurse so she could have the flexibility to take my siblings and I to various events and activities in the afternoon. When she moved into long-term care, she worked full time and part time simultaneously for years. Imagine clocking out from a stressful, unappreciative nine-to-five job on a Friday after working the entire week, only to take a nap and clock in to your weekend job at eleven pm—all while still having to maintain a household and raise kids. Mom did this for years. In retrospect, now as an adult, I can see how her working this hard and not ever feeling appreciated or content took a toll. I can understand how my parents ended up on this hamster wheel fighting to go in different directions.

When Devale and I embarked on our relationship with each other and at several points in our relationship, I clearly said, "Bro, if this is a space that you don't want to be in, please let me know that. Just be upfront and never take away my choice to decide whether or not I want to be here." I believe that this level of transparency and honesty has worked for us because there's a constant desire and a choice to want to be here. I don't feel like either of us is being held here against our will or that we are constantly worried about what other people are going to say. That is not a component in our relationship at all. I believe this is part of the reason we've been able to last. We've both been affected by seeing our parents just existing in their marriages. To me, living in a relationship out of obligation or keeping up appearances is toxic. I don't want my children anywhere near that kind of energy. So Devale and I are very purposeful about making sure we give each other the choice to be here every day.

Setting a New Example of Love

Devale

Watching my parents interact as I was growing up was interesting. As a child, I looked at my parents as if they were superheroes. I know everybody does. I thought that my parents could do nothing wrong. What I appreciated the most about my parents back then was the unified front that they put together against us as kids. My mom and dad had each other's backs like Bonnie and Clyde before I ever knew who Bonnie and Clyde were. It didn't matter if my dad was wrong, my mom would sit there and say, "What did your father say?" And vice versa.

Because my parents didn't argue in front of us, I didn't always know what was going on. So in those rare times when I would hear my parents arguing, I would immediately become very protective of my mother. Sometimes after those arguments, I would say to my Pops, "Why would you say that to Mom? That hurt her feelings." I remember him saying to me, "Boy, when you have your own family and your own wife, you'll understand as you get older."

I didn't understand in that moment, but I knew that he was not going to explain anything to me. I knew that he didn't feel he ever had to defend himself to me or anybody else about how he treated his wife and his kids. I watched my parents work hard to give me, my brother, Brian, and my sister, Tori, everything. But it was difficult to watch how some of their affection for each other disappeared as we got older. I remember when we lived in our first apartment in Flatbush, my mom would be cooking and my dad would hug her from behind and kiss her on her neck, or if he was being really playful, he would grab her butt. I remember being a young man and hearing from the radio, "This is 107.5, WBLS." The lights would be off in the living room, and Brian and I would sneak around to see what my parents were doing. I would love to see them slow dancing or cuddling on the couch. There were a few times when we got caught and I'd hear my father say, "Hey, get away from the door, go to your room."

As we got older, I watched how they became less affectionate, to the point where I don't know if my little sister ever saw them function as a loving couple. Throughout their marriage, I believe that my parents struggled with their communication, their Southern roots, and their connection to the Baptist church. Both my parents were raised by Southern parents and most of the Black couples they knew didn't get divorced. Which is crazy to me because my mom's parents got divorced and both remarried. But that's a story for a different book. For most Black families, there was no therapy or talking about their feelings. They just stayed together no matter what. While I know that my parents love each other, I rarely heard them compliment each other unless it was in a public forum.

Who wants to feel like a prisoner in their own home? Trapped with a nagging ungrateful spouse whose sole purpose is to make your life miserable? I for one knew that I would never sign up for that, and the more I looked at the married couples around me, that's all I saw. I've heard so many people say that growing up with married parents is the best way to learn how to be a married adult. Well, I beg to fucking differ.

My parents' generation was really never given the tools to effectively communicate with one another. Men were told to suppress their emotions and keep things from their wives, while wives were taught to be seen and not heard in the house. Husbands were taught that nagging wives were par for the course, and wives were taught that men will be men and wives should be grateful that they found husbands. These are definitely old stereotypical marriage tropes that more than likely come from the more discontented couples on the marriage spectrum, but this was the little bit of advice I received from those who were married before me. But I never subscribed to these ideas. Remember, I'm the "glass is half full" type of guy.

I was always determined to do marriage differently. I always dreamed of existing in a marriage with full transparency. I knew that I always wanted to create a safe space for my wife and me so that we could both feel free to tell each other exactly how we're feeling in real time. We are going to do our work together to discover how to be happy and thrive. The last thing I wanted to be was just another Black couple bickering and living miserably.

The only way I can be deliberate about trying to grow together with my wife is by continuing to learn, date, and court her. We hear that so many couples lose the courting and the dating process in their marriage. It's very easy to get lost in the thick of your career, your children, or health issues. There are so many things that could be a hindrance to maintaining that level of closeness and intimacy with your spouse. I've learned to be very deliberate about making sure that we continue to learn about each other and give ourselves the grace to take on life's inevitable changes.

Khadeen and I are not the same people we were when we met each other at eighteen. I've learned over time to stop expecting Khadeen to be who she was when I met her. I believe that holding on to those initial expectations is how people start to grow apart. Rather than talk about what you miss or need, people often withdraw and say, "I don't want to ruffle feathers, I'm just going to deal with these things my own way." From there, you start to see two people just fade into the abyss of relationship hell.

When you start to keep little things from your spouse, these small things end up becoming big things, like a wedge. It's a little point, and at the beginning it's very small, but as you continue to push forward, the bigger the issues get and the larger the space that is created between you and your spouse. I just choose to be deliberate about not wanting any wedges in between us.

Khadeen

Having our families around us in a healthy way is huge for Devale and me. There was a point where I wanted to make sure that Devale's mom was equally involved with our sons. We literally always had my mom over to help and we didn't see as much involvement with Devale's mom. At one point, he had a conversation with her because he was starting to feel like there was this imbalance in the kids being with my side of the family and not with his.

Fortunately, we were able to resolve that misunderstanding quickly. His mother gently explained, "I don't ever want to be considered to be the meddling or overbearing mother-in-law. I don't want to be that mother-in-law that y'all get tired of or that feels like she isn't wanted in your space because I've experienced that."

After having that conversation with his mom, it was just a matter of asking her and inquiring if she could help, and she was always ready to do so. We're at a space now where both families, whenever we need help, will pitch in. Devale thought it would be best for my mom to live with us in California, and he made provisions to be able to bring my parents along with us to our current home in Atlanta.

Now that we have four sons, it's a godsend to have both of my parents come with us. I wanted my sons to have the childhood memories that I had growing up with my grandparents. There's nothing like a grandparent's love, and I just love that my mom and dad are here with my children so that they can grow with them and have those memories because I know that they are not going to be around forever. It's also a great help to have extra people in the house.

Now I'm not gonna lie, we have had our moments where we had to figure out how to maintain boundaries with all these extra adults in the house. They've been doing a good job at trying to uphold whatever rules we have set in place with the children or just anything when it comes to day-to-day life. I'm grateful that my mom has repeatedly reiterated, "Khadeen, you are the lady of the house and what you want and what you say goes." Sometimes she has moments where she struggles with doing things the way she wants to do them or the way she sees fit. We've butted heads a few times, but I know that her advice and feedback is coming from a place of wanting to support me to be the best mother that I can be. There's an old West Indian saying, "Two women can't live in the same house." But we are making it work.

My parents are a blessing. I have friends who are unfortunately losing parents or the older relatives who raised them. I know that I am super blessed and fortunate to have my parents still here with me today. I don't take that for granted. Do they get on my nerves? Every single day, but I love them so, so much—and my kids adore them.

KHADEEN'S HOT TAKE
Family Boundaries

I am so grateful that Devale has been open to my mother living with us, first when we moved to Los Angeles and now that we are making our home in Atlanta. But let me tell you—getting two Caribbean women to live harmoniously under one roof has been some work. My mom will do something that is the total opposite of what I ask her to do, and she will defend herself by saying, "It's coming from a good place. I'm just trying to help." While I know her intentions are good, it's still overbearing at times. Even now with our youngest son, Dakota, she will check me if I am multitasking with him while I'm cooking or up-loading something to my phone or laptop. I kindly—yet forcefully—remind her that this is my *fourth* son and that I got it.

When you make this big decision to move in with fam-ily, you have to know the importance of boundaries—and be completely unapologetic about it. When it comes to establishing your limits with family, so many people are concerned about how the other person will receive it. Bro, sis, for real, let's stop doing that. We have to stop sacrific-ing the way we feel just to appease others. You are in con-trol of your own happiness—and you have to protect it at all costs. Maintaining your peace of mind is a vital form of self-care, and the sooner you realize that you have per-mission to put boundaries around your time and emo-tions, the sooner you'll be able to remove yourself from situations, even with family, that you have no place in.

DEVALE'S HOT TAKE
Family Boundaries

There are men who come up and ask me, "Yo, Devale, how is it living with your mother-in-law?" I know that I get that question a lot because it's commonplace to think that a mother-in-law will be naturally pushy or nosy or that you won't get along in general. For me and Khadeen's mom, Mimi, I believe the key to our relationship is that Mimi and I have come to know and respect each other's boundaries. Over time, she has really taken the time to help us with the boys and honor our need for privacy and space. But trust me, it didn't start this way.

When I first came around, Mimi was like a guard dog. Kay is her oldest child and of all her children, Kay was her prized possession. Khadeen was the ideal first child: winning pageants, graduating valedictorian, and being the most thoughtful big sister ever. She was headed off to college as this coddled little princess with no blemishes on her record and no real serious boyfriends her entire life up to that point. Then here I come. A confident, opinionated, self-aware athlete, with a loud car, shiny rims, an innocent smile, looking to smash.

If I'm being honest, that's all I was looking for at eighteen years old. Sue me.

Mimi was not having it. She literally tried everything to get Khadeen to believe that I was going to ruin her life. She even claimed I was gonna get Kay locked up for fraud one time because Kay had me say I was her father on the phone to AT&T so that she could clear up a phone bill that she ran up while talking to me during her family vacation. Mimi found a way to blame me for *everything*.

Once again, if I'm being honest, she wasn't exactly wrong. Kay got her first C ever *in life* in math as a sophomore in college because we would fuck, fall asleep, and miss our 2 p.m. class after common hour on Wednesdays. She got pregnant in college and had to have an abortion. She also put her TV career on hold for a year at age twenty-two to move to Detroit with me while I was playing for the Detroit Lions after she graduated from grad school magna cum laude. Fortunately, I turned out okay but it was touch and go for a minute for ya boy when it came to being on Mimi's good side. But that's what makes our love story that much greater.

There was a point in me and Kay's relationship when I refused to go to her parents' house because I felt like her mom was just plain mean and unbearable. It all came to a head one day when my father paid for a spring break trip for Kay and me to go to Jamaica. Kay lied to her mom and told her it was a group trip because she didn't want to tell her it was just the two of us going. Two weeks before the trip I begrudgingly went with Kay to her parents' house as she tried to subtly mention that all the other couples that were "supposed" to go with us backed out, but we still had to go because my dad had already paid for the trip.

Mimi was onto us and immediately pointed out that a girl of her "caliber" shouldn't be on a trip with some "bwoy." For all you non-Jamaicans, *bwoy* is a derogatory term used to describe a young man that is beneath you. I got up to walk out because I was going to get disrespectful and for the first time *ever* Kay stood up for me. They began to argue so I kissed Kay on the mouth and chucked the deuces. For two whole years I stayed away from Mimi because I didn't want to be disrespectful. I was never good at holding my tongue and I had a lot I wanted to let off my chest, but out of respect for Kay I never did. I knew I had to let time prove that I, like Mimi, wanted nothing but the best for Kay, and I was determined to show her that she was wrong about me.

When I look back on it now, as a father to my own children, I completely understand Mimi's concern, although I don't agree with her tactics to manipulate Kay into thinking I wasn't good enough for her. That hurt my feelings and if I didn't love and adore Kay the way I do, Kay would have missed out on the best thing to ever happen to her—and I would have missed out on it, too. But in the end patience and grace has allowed those wounds to heal and close.

So the thought and decision of living with my mother-in-law wasn't easy per se, but it hasn't been hard for me to adjust to living with Mimi because of the respect we've built for each other—and with that respect came lots of open communication and good conversations. The longer we live together, the more I appreciate that Mimi has come to understand who I am and how I want to continue to grow as a husband to Khadeen and as a father to my sons. Especially now with the addition of our fourth son, Dakota, our lives have become exponentially better because we consistently have an extra set of hands in the house to help Khadeen and me with the kids.

Living with your in-laws or other extended family members doesn't have to be a nightmare. Establishing good boundaries, sharing open communications, and having consistent check-ins will make all the difference in creating an atmosphere where you can come home to peace and harmony.

Khadeen

Right now, our middle son, Kairo, literally eats, sleeps, and breathes Devale. Anything Devale does, Kairo watches him like a hawk. Recently Devale said to our three oldest sons, "Listen, you got to look out for your mom. We got to protect the queen." Kairo took this charge to heart so seriously. On the nights that Devale is away, he literally does not leave my side. With the sincerest face, he looks at me and says, "Mommy, I have to take care of you. Daddy said so. Do you want something to drink? Do you want a head rub?" These are things that he's already seen Devale offer as acts of affection toward me. So it's super important for us to be able to do this on a public level and in private with our growing family. People need to know and be intentional and purposeful with their relationships. That's what we're hoping comes from our transparency and from us talking about our challenges and triumphs so publicly.

When Devale and I are apart, we literally can't wait to get back together. He could come home late at two or three in the morning and I will wait up for him. Devale is literally my homie. I'm a Sagittarius, and I certainly enjoy my alone time. However, if I had to pick a time to be with anybody else, it's going to be with him and then my boys.

We truly enjoy our time together. Even if it is something as mundane as going to Home Depot, one of us will inevitably say, "I'm coming with you!" When I have my moment alone, without fail, Devale will cuddle up with me and say, "Hey, I need more of you. I need to see you more." Sometimes I get wrapped up in my own world and three days might've passed and I hadn't been hanging with Devale as much as I know he needs me to. I'll have to just kind of circle back and be like "My bad, babe."

Now as a parent, I've also realized the value of living and existing within a healthy relationship so that our children can see it. That's why Devale and I are intentionally affectionate in front of our children. They will see us share a quick kiss or a booty grab and they know Mommy and Daddy do these things out of love. And of course, these public displays of affection are always accompanied by conversations about who you are allowed to be affectionate with. We are very deliberate about these talks with our boys.

I believe that generational cycles exist because no one's willing to speak about it, particularly in the Black and Caribbean families. No one wants to be transparent and honest, and as a result people suffer in silence for so long.

My family was never very affectionate physically. I can count the number of times my father said "I love you" or has given me a hug. As an older West Indian man, my father would show love by cooking my favorite meal because he knows that I love his curry eggplant, white rice, and dhal. That is how my father expressed his love. That is his love language and I've learned that its value isn't any less. In contrast, Devale and I have taken the approach where we try to show our children in so many different ways that we love and care for them. We want our children to see that not just from the parent-to-child perspective, but also in our relationship as husband and wife. We are their first example. We are who they want to emulate.

Devale

To me, setting a new example of love means being transparent and also vulnerable in my marriage. This practice empowers both Kay and me to grow; it has also been a form of therapy for me. It took time and work to go from worrying about being judged to learning to let go of what anybody thinks of me. It has been the most freeing aspect of my maturation, not only as a husband but as a man. Another thing I learned as an athlete: You have to let all previous plays go, whether bad or good. Having a short memory allows me to exist in the moment, focus on being better in the future, and not to hold my partner to previous expectations. I know that it's been therapeutic for me because I'm no longer hiding my imperfections. Marriage has taught me that you can't grow as a person or as a partner by trying to hide your imperfections and insecurities from the very person you have chosen to create a life with. You can only deal with your insecurities by putting them at the forefront and then saying "I've noticed this thing about myself. Let me work to be better at it." Sharing your insecurities can inspire your partner to be vulnerable and grow well. I know this because this is also something Kay has adopted over time.

I also realize that living in this truth has allowed me to be a testament to others. I know that my purpose on the planet is bigger than just surviving and getting more money. I'm here to share my life as a way to inspire other people. Whether you can learn something from me and say "I want to do something like Devale" or "I'm never doing that like Devale," both are a form of inspiration and it helps me feel I'm living my purpose. I'm truly enjoying that I can live a life with a partner in front of everyone, open and freely. I've just been blessed to find a partner who agrees that we want to share our life as a testament to what people can do and be if they choose to. That is the ultimate example of love.

Putting Friendship at the Core

Having a genuine friendship at the center of our marriage has given us a solid foundation to create longevity in our relationship. We know that our love story would not be two decades strong if we didn't genuinely respect each other, champion each other's goals, and work hard to create a future that we can be proud of for ourselves and our family. From our first date in college to thinking forward into our future as social media creators and entrepreneurs, none of this would be as fun, exciting, challenging, and enjoyable without seeing and valuing each other as friends.

How can you see your genuine care and affection for your partner when tensions are running high? Can you remember why you fell in love with them in the first place after a devastating loss or disappointment? Do you know how to fight fairly without pushing the wrong buttons or saying words that you will regret later on? Do you have the ability to still support the other person even after a soul-breaking transgression? For us, returning to our friendship, our commitment to each other, and our love for our sons always helps us to come back to home base.

These are the questions and observations that will help you to know whether your relationship is based on a solid friendship and if it will go the distance. In this chapter, we will explore what it looks like to weather the storms of a relationship and to keep friendship as the focus of your relationship.

Devale

Far too often, we put conditions on our marriages or relationships. In my opinion, this is typically how relationships become sour, because your partner isn't going to conform to all of your rules. That's not what I want in my marriage. I want a friend. I don't want a business partner who comes with guidelines. I don't want someone to tell me, "Here are the lists of rules for things I'm going to tolerate and not tolerate. You either fall in line or you keep it moving."

Nothing about our relationship is conventional. Yes, we honor and appreciate traditional standards, but when it comes down to rules and obligations, I treat Kay like she's my best friend—because she is. Not some pet I'm trying to train for a competition or show. I never wanted to have to jump through hoops to prove my love or have her do the same. I always wanted an unconditional, free-of-obligation love with a partner who chooses me every day on their own terms, because we are friends.

Khadeen and I have been broke together. We've been rich together when I was playing ball in the NFL and then back to broke when my career ended unexpectedly. Now we are experiencing a newfound wealth together. We've been through many aspects of life, but money comes and money goes. The only thing that has not changed in our relationship since we've been together is the fact that we enjoy each other's company. Companionship is probably the most invaluable thing in a relationship. There's nothing like waking up in the morning and knowing that someone has your back. There's no dollar amount you can put on that.

Khadeen

Friendship is the most important aspect of my marriage because—and it's going to sound clichéd—everything else is going to change or fade, no matter how hard you try. Ultimately, looks fade. It doesn't matter if they're going to fade thirty years from now or seventy years from now. At some point you're not going to look the same way you looked when you first met this person.

Over the years, we've evolved from having these heated

debates that would sometimes last the entire day. Now, with almost twenty years in, we will have a discussion, it'll be in real time, and then we keep it pushing. We don't have any time or any desire to continue to linger in the state of unrest. We resolve the issue the best we can by striving always to understand the other person's viewpoint.

I've tried to employ a lot of the same tactics that Devale and I use when it comes to my parents and my siblings now. It's helpful that my brother and sister are open to being effective communicators and talking about the way they feel. My brother still tries to avoid whatever issue has come up (we called it the "Ostrich Technique" in my family), but my sister and I tend to be more vocal. I've seen how my parents, particularly my mom, can sometimes be taken aback by my forwardness now. With a Jamaican mom, you have to tread lightly and be careful about your tone and the way you say things. Even with me almost pushing forty, the level of respect that I have for my mother is something that cannot be overlooked, and I would never do or say anything to disrespect her or my dad.

However, I have noticed that my forwardness is sometimes met with a little bit of combativeness. My mother will be quick to say, "I can't believe you're saying that to me." As the oldest of six children, my mother has always been the person to check someone or to be the leader because she's the oldest. Since I'm also the oldest child, I get it, too. Someone who's used to always checking somebody is not used to being checked. So when I have to confront my mom on things from time to time, she may take it as me trying to be combative or trying to disrespect her. I've had to let her know that this is just me trying to be as transparent as possible, because over the years the silent route has not worked.

Over the years, my parents have often made comments about how great Devale and I are doing or how well we're able to work together. I often reply by saying, "This is largely in part because we communicate, we discuss things, and we're moving in one accord." Improving my communication with Devale has definitely helped when it comes to my extended family. At this point, my parents understand this is just Khadeen standing in her womanhood and wanting the best for everybody. I've recently witnessed my parents still having the same issues with no resolution and hearing the same problems from when I was a teenager. Seeing that there's been no progress over many decades can be very disheartening and frustrating.

That is why Devale and I were united in not ending up like either one of our parents. Don't get me wrong. Our parents have been wonderful providers. But looking at them through the lens of a married woman, I can really see where there was a disconnect over the years, and that's something Devale and I are trying to avoid at all costs. It really took a lot for us to learn how to communicate our needs and desires. Devale and I never stop talking about what we want and need.

We've learned that everything is not going to be a strategically planned-out argument of how we're going to arrive at a certain answer or how we're going to sleep tight and be all happy. But sometimes we know how to table the discussion, pick our battles, and just move on. Effective communication has been an ongoing process for us that we continue to work on to this day.

Devale

When Khadeen and I first started dating, both of us were eighteen. I remember feeling like Khadeen was on a completely different planet. I didn't understand how she moved the way she moved. For example, I'm big on dealing with things up front. If I have an issue with you, I want to sit down and I want to talk about it. I want to make sure that we both understand each other so we can move forward. With Khadeen, every time I tried to sit down and have a conversation with her, she just got very quiet and then very defensive.

Whenever I tried to point out something to Khadeen, she would stop talking. It took me five years (yes, five whole fucking years!) before I realized, "Hmm, maybe this is a family dynamic thing." I point out the time because we as people have become so accustomed to technology providing instant gratification or results, that we see any extended process as failure. Most people are not persistent enough to get the results they desire. I only had this realization when I started to really get to know Khadeen's parents and her brother and sister. I noticed that everyone in her family had the same response to criticism. When you say something to them, their first instinct is to get quiet. Then they defend their right to feel the way they feel as opposed to saying "Maybe I could have done this differently."

In my family, I was always on the opposite end of the criticism. For thirty to forty-five minutes each month we would talk about everything from our attitudes to our chores, how late we were staying up, and when our parents were disappointed with our behaviors.

As a young Ellis, if you were a child in the house, you had no right to respond or say what your thoughts were on it. The minute you tried to respond, you were considered a bad apple or had a poor attitude. But that didn't stop me from talking back and my parents from telling me that my attitude stinks. When I got over my attitude, I did try to understand where my parents were coming from so that I could make the changes. I grew up believing that my family's way was the right way because I achieved certain successes in life, even though I often left those meetings feeling beaten down.

But when I moved out of my parents' house, I no longer had to worry about that. When I started dating Khadeen, I naively thought that all families operated the same way. Boy, was I dumb!

I thought that because we were both the oldest of three children and that she grew up with both of her parents, our communication styles would be compatible. I'll never forget the holiday season of 2003. Khadeen and I actually grew up seven blocks from each other in Canarsie, so splitting time during the holidays should be simple, right? *Wrong!* We decided to go to her family's house first on Thanksgiving Day because my parents went to my aunt Debbie's house in Flatbush. Kay's grandmother, aunt, and uncle live a block and a half from her parents, so her family decided to meet there for dinner. She and I drove from Hofstra that day to spend the holiday with both families.

We got to Grandma Joseph's house in the early evening and waited for her family to sprinkle in and bless the food. By the time everyone came and Khadeen was ready to go, it was minutes to eleven o'clock. I was not having the best time because I felt like Kay had forgotten that we still had to drive to Flatbush to see my family. Kay's family was in full holiday mode. All her cousins and the other family members were having drinks and telling stories, so Kay was not ready to leave, but she could sense my attitude and prepared to go anyway. We said our goodbyes to everyone, which took another twenty minutes, and finally left.

It was an extremely quiet car ride to Flatbush, to say the least, but we finally arrived close to midnight and half my family had already left. My parents were already back home in Canarsie and all my cousins had already dispersed for the after-dinner activities. I was livid. We stayed for a few minutes, then drove back to Kay's family's house for the remainder of the night.

On the car ride home, I straight up told Khadeen that I felt like she was selfish and completely disregarded my family for hers. I kept asking her how she could think it was fair to spend hours with her family knowing that I was away from mine on the holiday. She had no answer. I kept asking her why she'd insisted we go to her family's house so early if she knew they would be there so late into the night. She had no answer. I became so frustrated by the lack of communication that I started talking out loud to myself and proclaiming that I would never split the holidays ever again. She stayed quiet the whole time until tears fell from her eyes.

I didn't understand what was going on. We literally did everything she wanted to do and she's still crying. I was now pissed and confused, but the sight of her crying in the passenger seat broke me. I instantly stopped talking about dinner and kept asking what was wrong. All she said was "Nothing."

I soon discovered that she had grown up completely differently from me. I had to figure out very early that the way I communicated turned her off because she felt attacked all the time. The minute she felt attacked, she would immediately stop listening to whatever I was saying. It took me five years to realize that I had become my parents, and my communication style often left Kay feeling beaten down just like I felt after an Ellis family caucus. Guys, if you think your lady is so hard to understand, dig a little deeper into why she might be acting a certain way. She's not your adversary, she's your friend.

Khadeen

Communication was very difficult for us in the beginning. But we were committed to being on this learning curve together because we wanted to do better and really understand each other. The desire to want to grow is what helped us navigate communication a lot better, considering my background with my family. There is also a bona fide desire to truly unpack each other's feelings. This is the only way to move forward and progress with your partner at the forefront.

When we first started dating, it all came down to communication styles. I didn't come from a house with very vocal parents. My parents would just dodge whatever they were at odds about until it went away, or so they thought. We all knew that whatever the issue was, it never really went away. So for days and sometimes for weeks at a time, there would be these festering, lingering problems that never got resolved. Even if the issue was discussed later, the wheels were never set in motion to change the behavior or address the issue.

I can't even call what my parents did miscommunication because they didn't communicate. They just existed as two separate people. When Devale and I started dating, it was difficult because every time he attempted to have a conversation with me, I would just shut down. I wasn't used to being vocal, particularly in a relationship. I had never really seen it happen.

One thing Devale would always say to me is "I just want you to understand where I'm coming from." I would often fire back, "That's fine and dandy, but I also need you to understand why I might have done a particular thing or set a particular action into place." I needed to unpack how I arrived at my decision, and most times, he didn't even care about what I did or how I got there. He just wanted to be understood. I would most times get caught up in defending my point and we'd end up on these exhausting tangents and forget what we were discussing to begin with.

Devale

I treated Khadeen the way I was treated as a person because I thought that that was a healthy way of communicating. When my parents or my coaches had an issue with me, they would sit me down and tell me what was wrong. Even more so as an athlete, I would be forced to sit and look at game-day films that pointed out all my flaws. Because of my successes in life I assumed that this way of communicating was the only way to build a person. It was always about accountability and being able to focus on the things you as an individual can control. That was my process. Show me what I did wrong so that I can fix it, and I'll do the same for you.

That approach backfired with Khadeen—hard. It was counterproductive because when Khadeen was presented with accountability she felt attacked. Then she would often feel like she was inadequate. She would tell me later that she felt bad because she could never reach this gold standard that I had created for what I envisioned from my girlfriend at the time.

It was also hard on me because I wasn't communicating effectively. I probably didn't learn until my late twenties how detrimental, toxic, and misaligned my communication methods were. I soon discovered that I can't speak to everyone like a coach. I can't speak to everyone like I'm a parent and they're a child. That's going to turn people off and your message will get lost in translation.

The only way Khadeen and I got through our communication differences was through trial and error. She and I have never been through therapy together. I went to therapy on my own for a little while later in our marriage. Realistically I learned the most by communicating directly with my wife and watching her. When I say "communicating," I don't mean talking at her or really even talking at all. I had to understand how to actively listen to what she's saying and how she's saying it.

Trust me, I tried many different ways to communicate. I even did the whole "walking on eggshells" thing, but that didn't work. I did the whole "don't communicate and let them figure it out" thing, but that was a fail, too. I went through so many different methods to discover what worked for Khadeen. I learned that there's no way to sit down and tell someone, "This kind of communication should work best for you." But if you love this person and you want to build a life together, it's worth putting in the work to understand them. That is the key. Learning to listen for understanding as opposed to listening to respond. Communication is not one-sided. That's why we have one mouth but two ears.

We all have different backgrounds. We all see things through a different lens and have different perspectives. For Khadeen and me, even with the hard bumps, I didn't mind putting in the work because I knew she was going to do her part, too. It took a shit ton of time to get there, but it was worth it. We finally got to a point where we didn't have to have drag-out arguments where we were disrespectful or intentionally hurtful to each other.

One of the funniest experiences we had early on in our communication styles was in 2004. Khadeen and I had been dating for two years and Facebook was just becoming popular for college students. I remember Khadeen being upset with me because a young lady sent me a Facebook message that said something like "Hey, Devale! Great game!" Nice, right? Immediately Khadeen said, "Why you got these hos in your inbox?" So I was just like "That's interesting. Why she got to be a ho? You sent the same message to your resident who plays basketball . . . I guess you are okay with displaying ho-like behavior."

Fast-forward another two hours, we end up arguing about the tone that we used when using the word *ho*. Khadeen felt that me saying "ho-like behavior" was condescending on top of the fact that the word *ho* was already disrespectful. We ended up arguing for seven hours. We both went to sleep, and when we woke up the next day, we were both still pissed about Facebook messages.

What I realized in that moment is that when you argue with your significant other, you will spend more time arguing and debating about how to argue and debate than the actual issue. As a person who has been in a relationship for over twenty years, I will say 85 percent of our arguments have not been about what spawned the argument. It's been about how we talk to each other while debating.

Life can be heavy at times. Having a friend that you can smile with through the ups and downs of life is what it's all about. I've learned that an unconditional friendship has no ceiling. People who have unconditional friendships can be friends forever, regardless of what happens. They can disagree on things. They can do stuff accidentally to hurt each other. But if you have a strong friendship, you'll come back if proper communication is available.

I want a friend who's going to work with me to create an experience in life together that works for both of us. The only way you can do that is if you start with an unconditional friendship that will last. Because let me tell you something about this thing called life and marriage: Shit is going to happen. If you don't have the ability to give grace, be forgiving and be understanding, you ain't never going to make it through. Proper communication doesn't end with you getting your point across—that's merely the beginning. The other part of the process is being able to listen to your partner's perspective without judgment of how your partner is communicating. Grace and time are needed to learn each other's communication styles.

Khadeen

Over time, we learned how to debate and reconcile by dropping our egos. At times we've had to sit down and agree, "Baby, this is stupid. We're arguing about something that's not going to affect or change what we really want from each other. We're arguing about something so trivial and we're wasting time that we'll never get back. Let's really focus on the task at hand." We are now more forgiving in how we speak to each other when we're emotional and upset. We give each other more grace and space. As humans, we might say something wrong or interpret something out of context. But as we've matured and grown with each other, we're more attuned to how we receive information from each other and seek to understand where we are both coming from before we respond.

We also learned over time to notice each other's triggers and not use them to win arguments. At that point, it wasn't about being right. It was about making the other person be more upset so you can feel like you won—which is the most immature thing ever.

But when you're young and in love, and no one has given you the tools for how to be successful in a relationship, these are the things that you think will help you win. But as you get older, you realize that nobody wins when you go to bed tired, angry, and frustrated. You realize that you're just wasting time with the person you want to love and spend the rest of your life with.

It really was an epiphany for both of us that so many of our arguments were stupid. Our days on earth are numbered, so why continue arguing about things that aren't going to help either one of us be better?

Devale is hands down my best friend and we've even joked sometimes and said, "If we weren't together for whatever reason, we would probably still be best friends. And whoever we move on to be with will just have to understand that we're just going to be best friends." People say all the time, "You can't choose family, but you can choose friends to be like family." There's no obligation when it comes to a friendship, or at least the friendships I choose to engage in.

The thing that I love the most about my friendships, and of course from Devale being my best friend, is that there's a choice to be involved in these relationships. There aren't any real conditions to being this person's friend. It's something that happens very organically. It happens without coaxing or having to try too hard. There's also a genuine level of understanding that seems to happen with my friendships. I can talk to some of my friends today and I won't have to speak to them for six months. Then we pick right up where we left off. That best friend component that I have with Devale is just an effortlessness that comes with our relationship. We've grown to where we can just have so much fun doing the most random things.

Even when things get tough, I now know how to step away from the role of parent, or business partner, or even as a spouse and tell him, "I miss my friend." Back in college, we would have the most fun just hanging out in my apartment, playing cards, getting food from the student cafeteria, and taking an occasional road trip when we had a long weekend. Now that we have four sons, our lives will never be that simple again. So we have to remind each other to go back to those basics when we fall off track. It happens, life happens, but we can choose to not just allow life to happen to us.

Even though we have so many other things going on right now, going back to those roots is so important for us. I believe that our friendship being at the core of our relationship has kept our marriage strong. So take the time to build that friendship—it will result in a relationship built on mutual trust and respect.

Doing the Work

It's really popular for people to say "You gotta do the work." But what does that mean? And whose work exactly are you doing? Is it the work of being better parents? Is it the work of supporting each other's dreams? For us, we discovered that our work was truly making our relationship service-based to each other instead of ego-based about our individual needs and wants. Having good communication in our relationship has been essential to helping us discover our goals: making sure that each of our dreams has a solid focus, that our sons are set up for a healthy future, and that we are establishing a firm legacy that we can be proud of.

Are you prepared to do the work that is required to help your relationship go the distance? Are you good within yourself to take the spotlight off yourself and allow your partner to be the focus? It's time to get your hands dirty and open up your hearts to discover what the work is for you and your partner and how to make sure that each of you gets the results that you want out of your relationship. Remember this, good work requires failure. Failing your partner is never the end unless you quit. We all learn our most valuable lessons through our biggest failures. But the greatest apology for an epic fail is always changed behavior.

Khadeen

When I look back through our twenty years, Devale being cut from the NFL was probably one of the biggest points in our relationship where I felt we were either going to sink or swim. We were either going to be together long-term or we were going to break things off. Devale came to me randomly after four years and said that he didn't want to play anymore. This was random because he asked me to trust him during this process and we had a financial plan that involved him playing ball. I put my career on hold to be what he needed during that process and we hadn't yet reached our financial goal for him to transition out of football. I felt betrayed. At this point, I was twenty-six years old with very little work experience in my field, but I could have just scrapped this whole thing, and focused on my needs.

This one moment in our relationship was going to be the microcosm of the rest of our relationship. We needed to find a way to reconcile and decide if we wanted to still be together or not, because it was now or never. I had to let him know how I felt, and he let me know how he felt. We were able to have a candid, adult conversation.

When Devale was first signed as a free agent into the NFL and began playing for the Detroit Lions, we were often at odds. He told me that he felt I wasn't understanding of the fact that he was by himself in Michigan. I told him that I didn't think he was understanding of the fact that I was dealing with being alone in graduate school. This was the first time in our relationship that distance was our reality and we missed each other so much. We ultimately understood that we were dealing with things differently.

All I could hear is my mom's voice in my head telling me that I needed to focus on my career and not be too quick to run behind Devale—who was already successful in his NFL journey. I didn't view my desire to "run behind him" as insecurity or immaturity. We struggled because our college years seemed to create a codependency that we could not shake. Devale could not function 100 percent without me and I couldn't without him. Looking back, we may have had an unhealthy reliance on each other but it felt harmless in the moment. We worked better together and something as major as making it pro was something we wanted to fully experience together. This shift felt crippling at times.

Through this breakdown, we were able to understand how the other dealt with change because that was the first big change that we had had in our relationship.

Devale

When I first got to Detroit, I was struggling big time. This was the first time I was away from my family, my friends, and most importantly my Kay Kay. The truth is, I didn't know how to adjust to my life in Michigan and neither did she. The NFL experience is tough as it is (that's a whole other book) but I was an undersize, free agent tryout guy that was physically and mentally drained. I developed an addiction to pain meds and was dealing with a number of injuries throughout my rookie season. I numbed my pain with alcohol and pain meds; she numbed hers by spending time out with her friends. At the time I was pissed. I felt that I was putting my body on the line and in isolation to build this dream life we both desired while she was back in New York having hot-girl weekends. I didn't know that she was just going out because being in her apartment while I was in Detroit just reminded her that I wasn't there.

When I first got back at the end of the season, I was in a terrible mental place. I was sleeping all day, then waking up to do shots of Patrón with my buddies who had just completed their rookie seasons as well. We were supposed to be celebrating, but I was using this time to catch up on all the partying I thought Kay was doing while I was working. I was staying with Kay in her campus apartment but staying out all night with my boys just to be petty. I thought doing this to her would make her see how I felt the four months I was in Detroit waiting for her to call me at two and three in the morning after being out all night with her friends, knowing that I had to be up for practice at six o'clock. But all it did was make shit worse. She and I fought constantly, and more importantly, I wasn't feeling any better about anything. I had to learn how to be forgiving and give Khadeen grace, because me doing something on purpose to hurt her is way worse than her accidentally doing something to make me feel bad. That was a tipping point for me.

One of the biggest lessons I learned during that time was, you guessed it, how important it is to communicate. Have you noticed a trend? I assumed that Kay was just out enjoying her life because she was free from being with me. I never asked why she went out so often. I just projected my insecurities onto her and created any narrative I could to justify that uncomfortable feeling I had. I was alone. It didn't matter to me what Khadeen was doing at the time. I just wanted to be a part of the decision-making process. I wanted to have a choice. Every time Kay did something for herself and I wasn't included, I felt as if I wasn't a priority and I didn't matter. I never considered that she could be struggling with the distance as well and trying to find a way to cope.

When you make decisions in your life for yourself and you're choosing to have a partner, your choices, your decisions, and your words matter. You have to continue to be of service to someone when you choose to be in a relationship. At any point you can leave, but when you decide that you want to be there, you're choosing to be of service to that person. If you're choosing to be there *and* not being of service to that person, you're doing more harm than good. That conduct can be detrimental to their mental health and can make their life miserable, and it's unfair to do that to anyone.

Our first year apart was extremely difficult. For the first time in my life, I didn't have my parents, my brother, my sister, or Khadeen. I was on an island by myself. This was the first time in my life when I was living in a different state with a completely different team. And because the NFL was never the final dream for me, I was inwardly focused on a completely different goal.

I hadn't planned on how to navigate this different step in my life, and now I had to do it by myself. It was difficult for me because I didn't know how to take care of myself. Because I was so goal-oriented, I would wake up, not eat breakfast, and just go straight to practice.

Khadeen was still getting her master's degree and was a resident director at Hofstra, and some days ran late for her. But we made an agreement that she would send a picture of herself every evening. If I got out of practice at nine o'clock, checked my email, and there was no picture, it would put me in the worst mood ever. On top of that, when you're playing in the NFL, after the first week of camp, 99 percent of the people are hurt or have endured some kind of injury. I was no different.

I started to develop a dependency on pain meds to get

through practice. I started taking four Tylenol in the morning, four more before practice, and four more after practice. Then I would take two Vicodin and go to sleep.

That dependency started to make me real moody, although I didn't realize I had a dependency at the time. But the minute I would get out of practice, if I didn't see the picture, I would get pissed. I would call Khadeen and then we would end up in a shouting match.

The dream was for me to at least make the practice squad for the Detroit Lions, earn $100,000 between September to December, come back home, and use that money to buy a two-family house. My plan was for us to rent out the upstairs part of the house to cover the mortgage and we would live downstairs and focus on our dreams of TV and film.

I was focused on being the one in our relationship who was taking the beating for this master plan. Therefore, I expected Khadeen to do her part and just check in with me on a daily basis. Now I can see that by being away from my family and living in a different environment, I was building up an enormous amount of stress.

One night always stands out for me because of the domino effect that followed. Kay used to party every Thursday, Friday, and Saturday nights when I was in Detroit. She used to drive to Brooklyn and hang out with her cousin Sophia and friend Lisa. One time she called me and said that a guy had her double-parked in and wouldn't let her leave unless she gave him her number. Of course I was pissed because I was all the way in Detroit and could not do anything to help, but ultimately he let her out and she was on her way to drop Lisa at home before heading back to Hofstra.

Every night when Kay was out, I would wait up by the phone to ensure that she was safe, even though I had practice early in the morning. Well, this one night in particular, I got no call or text from Kay. I called Lisa, but Lisa said the same thing. She hadn't heard from Kay since being dropped off. Now I'm panicking, but still have to go to practice, so in between meetings I'm checking my phone. I start to receive texts and calls from both her mom and mine that no one has seen or heard from Kay since the night before.

At this point my mom calls and says she thinks I should come home. I assume the worst and break down crying in the locker room. In my mind, they found Kay and don't want to tell me over the phone. NFL security gets involved and begins a probe to help find Kay. Hofstra security breaks into her apartment to see if she was there—and nothing. No sign of Kay anywhere. I'm calling her phone nonstop for hours with no response. Finally, the team gets me a flight to head back to New York.

I'm at the airport still calling Kay's phone, but now it's going to voice mail and I'm trying to hold it together. That's when it happened. My phone rings and it's Kay's number. I answer expecting to hear someone give me a demand for ransom, but nope, it's Kay. "Hey, babe! What's going on?" she asked. The relief I felt when I heard her voice was quickly crushed by embarrassment at the thought of everything that had transpired that morning. I had just broken down in an NFL locker room. The team had to get the league's security involved. Hofstra had to break into her apartment, all because she chose to stop at her aunt's house to sleep and forgot her phone in the car. I was livid. I never got on the plane to go back home. Instead I had to go back to practice and deal with a locker room full of grown men ready to laugh at the rookie who lost it because he didn't hear from his girlfriend overnight. If you are wondering how that felt, just imagine being a high school freshman and getting called up onstage at assembly with the prettiest girl and having an erection in front of the whole school. It was one thousand times worse than that. And I blamed Kay for all of it.

Khadeen

That first year apart was a learning experience for us, because we were now experiencing what it was like to be together but also have distance between us. Not only that, but Devale was now going to be in the NFL in a different state.

There were so many different thoughts and assumptions that were being poured into our minds. As much as we tried to tune it out, we still had lingering suspicions about what would potentially happen now that we had nothing but time, distance, and opportunity between us. As much as I wanted to be there for Devale and be in the same space with him, I just couldn't do that and maintain my school schedule. Devale also had a very rigid schedule with the NFL with required practices and game days. It was the first time that we had some boundaries that we couldn't control, just because that was our life at the time.

At some points, I felt like Devale expected me to bend the rules and find a way to make things happen around my school schedule. There were times where he didn't necessarily respect the fact that I had stuff going on, too. I often felt obligated to figure out how to make things more comfortable for him because he was feeling so isolated and out of touch with his life back home.

One night in particular, he popped up on text and demanded, "Yo, I need you to send me pictures TONIGHT." I was in the middle of a residential-life training and I texted back, "I can send them to you on my next break." He immediately fired back, "NO. I need you to send me a picture NOW." I spent more than a few nights beefing with him that first summer if I was late sending him pictures. And this was in the late 2000s, well before FaceTime or being able to take a quick selfie on your phone. I would literally have to set up a physical camera, use the reflection in the mirror, upload the picture to my laptop, and *then* send it to him. It was insane!

I know now that he was just worried about how he was going to get by, but I was also dealing with the stresses of not having him close by. I was trying to be understanding of the fact that he had this new life to acclimate to. Adjusting to our new lives was hard for us to deal with and the distance just made it that much worse.

Devale

The lowest point for me during this time was when I returned to New York after my rookie season. I made the team and earned a whole lot of money, but I wasn't happy. Football for me was just a means to an end. My goal was to prepare myself for life after football. During this time, I had a lot of resentment around feeling like Khadeen was not putting in the same amount of work that I was putting in.

Rather than constantly call Khadeen and badger her into doing what I wanted her to do, I started to move differently. When I first came back home to New York, I had developed my own routine at this point. I was a "rich rookie" who had just earned two hundred and fifty thousand dollars and now I had all the time in the world. In the NFL between January and March, most new players like me had absolutely nothing to do. I would party as late as four in the morning, sleep until three in the afternoon, and start drinking the minute I woke up. This routine was my way of dulling the pain of withdrawing from my pain meds. When I wasn't feeling well, I would grab a vodka and orange juice or a Hennessy and Coke, then connect with my boys, and we would party all night.

There was one night during this time where I woke up in

a cold sweat and I was shivering uncontrollably. All I could do was collapse on the bathroom floor and cry. Fortunately, Khadeen was with me that night and she called my receiver coach, Jamie Elizondo. That night on my bathroom floor, he and I had the realest conversation I had had to this point in my life. Jamie was a Bible-believing man and he simply said to me, "Devale, you are living a dream that many people don't get a chance to live. You need to get it together and man up. You need to pray and figure out what strength you need in order to get through this. Ask God to help you and you need to take the time to figure out how to be a better man for Khadeen."

The accountability that my coach and Khadeen provided to me in that moment was exactly what I needed to hear. It no longer mattered how much money I had in the bank if I didn't know how to treat the woman I loved. I didn't want to wake up and be unhappy every morning because I didn't know how to manage my emotions and be the man I needed to be on and off the field. Plain and simple, I had to learn how to manage my addiction and put a stop to my drinking immediately. That night on the bathroom floor, I made the decision that I was going to do it—and I did.

It wasn't easy. I found that I was never given the skills to manage my emotions. If there's one thing that my father never spoke to me and my brother about, it was about emotions. We talked about finances, manhood, providing and protecting our women, but we never ever talked about having control over our emotions. As a young, immature man, all I could do when I felt uncomfortable was to blame the closest person to me, and I was wrong to do that. I had to put in the work to get myself in the right place before I could get better.

Khadeen

The lowest point during this whole first year apart was definitely when Devale and I were coexisting in my apartment together and literally living as strangers. I was in graduate school and I had an apartment on campus. Technically Devale did not have a place to stay when he came back from the NFL. I felt like I had some leverage with being the leaseholder for the apartment and having the ability to kick him out if I wanted to.

I struggled during that time because part of me felt better knowing that he was in the same space as me. I felt comfort in knowing that he was around, even though I was upset and hurt by his actions. He was doing his own thing and I was doing my own thing. I knew that I could have asked him to just leave altogether and he'd have to find somewhere to go or go back to his parents' house in Brooklyn until it was time for him to leave again.

But I knew deep down that I did not want him to go. I felt we were wasting so much time that we could have spent bonding, having quality time together, and loving on each other. But here we were in the same space at odds with each other and constantly fighting.

Our age was definitely showing there, because the Devale and Khadeen who can communicate now, twenty years later, were not the Devale and Khadeen during that winter of 2007. There was a lot of noncommunication happening because we were constantly mad at each other and we both had points to prove.

I was just putting up a facade at the time because I felt I had to. I had to put my foot down because how dare he come back from Michigan, stay in my apartment, eat my food, benefit from living with me, and be out there just doing whatever he wants to do. He wasn't going to make me look stupid coming back on campus now, hanging out with his boys and whatever girls were on campus, and then coming back to sleep in my apartment.

When I told him he had to leave one night, he bundled up in his bubble coat and black scarf, and he packed up this suitcase that he brought from Michigan. He looked as sad and lost as Mary J. Blige in her "Not Gon' Cry" video. He was very defiant that day and he was like "You're not telling me to leave. I'm leaving because I want to leave."

As much as I wanted to hold my ground, I yelled at his back as he was leaving, "Where are you going to go now? Are you going to find a way to get back to Brooklyn to go to your parents' house? Are you going to bunk up with one of your old roommates? How is that going to work?"

When Devale left with that suitcase, he was gone for all of thirty minutes and then he came back. He stomped back inside and said, "I'm going to stay here, but I'm not going to stay with you. I'm going to stay in the other room." I was being equally petty and replied, "I don't want you to stay in the room with me anyway." I was still angry at him, but part of me still felt a little bit of a relief.

We spent weeks being petty and I started to get a little bit of anxiety at this point because I knew it was leading up to the time when he was going to have to go back to Detroit for training camp. I was upset, to the point where it was making me physically ill. I was kicking myself because I felt we were wasting so much time arguing and bickering. I was slowly thinking, "At any moment he's going to be going back to Detroit for spring training and we're going right back to not being together again." This was the first time in our relationship that I felt it would either make or break us.

When I look back at that time, I now understand even more the value of being honest and the value of being transparent. Even though it may hurt the other person's feelings, or it might feel like an uncomfortable situation, we wasted so much time when we could have been loving on each other and enjoying each other's company. We could have been doing that with a simple, honest conversation.

Now, I believe that this is why Devale and I are able to get past things where we may have a disagreement. It's a lot easier for us to do that now because we don't take things personally. This is a lesson that I also picked up from rule number two in the book *The Four Agreements*. You have to also understand that sometimes your intention is not the way things are received. We both felt that even though our intentions might have been good, it really wasn't okay for the other person.

I'm glad that we can laugh now at all the stupid things that we might have said to each other and the stupid things that we did. I know ultimately it makes for a great story because here we are today. Now, being apart for longer stretches of time is no big deal for us because we have learned how to effectively communicate with each other. You might find that once you are willing to put in the work to understand your partner, little things don't blow up into bigger issues because you have no problem talking something out and working your way to a good solution.

Devale

For a single person reading this book, my first piece of advice is to honestly ask yourself, "Do I want to be in a relationship?" This is a very important question. Many people don't know what a good relationship entails. Far too often, people are seeking what they see on television or what they've witnessed in their parents', friends', or other family member's relationships.

You also have to be willing to ask yourself, "Do I want to be of service to someone else for the rest of my life?" and

"Am I willing to rely on that person to be of service to me?" Once you make that decision, you have to commit 100 percent. This is my definition of what a truly monogamous relationship is. A relationship that's healthy happens without conditions. You and your spouse or partner have to decide to come together and try to figure out life together. I'm emphasizing the phrase "try to figure out life," because the truth is, we are all out here guessing. Nobody has it figured out. Khadeen and I don't have it figured out. None of your favorite couples have it figured out. You won't know what a successful relationship is until you do the work to figure it out for yourself.

Kay and I were able to resolve our issues in 2007 by dropping our egos first. I was an egotistical, maniacal, immature, broken, and hurt young man with a lot of money and time on my hands. I realized that in the moments I was getting ready to leave to go back to Detroit that none of the money I had, "friends" hanging around, or women interested could take that place of peace that only Kay provided. I chose that moment to relinquish the control my ego had over my emotions and just be honest with Kay. I stopped telling myself that being vulnerable would give her the upper hand and told her exactly how I felt about everything for the first time. For the first time, she told me about everything she was going through while I was gone. We both felt so dumb, but it was the most freeing moment of my life because that weight of having to be in control was finally lifted, and that isolation I put myself in no longer existed. This narrative I had created about what Kay was doing and how she was living was all an illusion created by stress and insecurities. It was all self-inflicted, but correctible.

DEVALE'S HOT TAKE
Commitment

You have to be willing to be in a relationship when the person is not meeting your expectations. You have to hang in there when situations change. That thing you thought you wanted one day may completely change tomorrow. If you choose to be with this one person for the rest of your life, you have to deal with them through the ups and downs. You learn to love them as they evolve as people. You must be willing to embrace change and enjoy the journey. With monogamy there is no final destination, because people exist in a constant state of evolution.

Ultimately, if monogamy doesn't sound like an arrangement you want to be in on a daily basis, that's okay, too. You can still live a full, healthy life and not need to be bogged down by the social constructs that we've created as people. Monogamy, truth be told, is not the only answer to love. There are so many other options to love, and monogamy is just one of those choices.

But if you really want to know if you are equipped for a

monogamous relationship, I challenge you to see if you can love someone unconditionally and without obligation, as long as it is not to the detriment of your physical or mental health or the health of others. Once you are confident that you are in a safe, secure, and loving relationship, be open to loving someone regardless of what they do, how they speak, how they act, or what choices they make. If they love you the same way unconditionally, they will never intentionally do anything to hurt you or repeat behaviors that don't consider you as well. If you can find someone you love like that, and that person can love you the same way, that's a real couple's goal.

Khadeen

Single people who want to be in a monogamous relationship need to understand that a monogamous relationship means that you are one with that person. You are committed to working together to coexist, grow, and build your personal and collective goals within your relationship. You have to come into the relationship with a mindset of knowing that it's no longer just about you and what you desire.

Now I'm not telling you to suppress your feelings and desires in order to be in a monogamous relationship. Not at all. In fact, you must be willing to openly express what you feel, need, and desire honestly and in real time. Vulnerability is a must and guardedness will only create barriers that encourage heartache—not prevent it. However, you have to take into account how that other person will feel. Be open to hearing their feelings, needs, and desires without judgment if they may not be in alignment with yours at that moment. It's no longer just making that singular decision that you think is in your best interest. Sometimes it requires taking a whole 360-degree view of what that decision may look like and how it's going to impact your significant other.

Being in a monogamous relationship is all about selflessness. If that's not something you desire, get out and save yourself and the other person the heartache. You have to be clear about your intentions, your wants, and your desires. Take the guessing out of the equation. When you take the guessing off the table, everyone comes to the relationship on a level playing field and then each person is free to make a choice from there.

Remember back in the Introduction when we said that you have to be in love with the idea of marriage? It's a 'hood we have to want to visit—and live in. If you were never the "marriage type" or don't see yourself as someone who could settle down with one person, you can't expect that someone will come along and completely change your ideology. That puts all of the pressure on the other party involved to be this picture-perfect person who needs to maintain a moment as a standard. What happens when this person changes? What if he or she is no longer "doing it for you?" I have experienced interactions with couples—some of whom have been married, divorced, and never desired to marry again. And I know others who have been married say they would never marry again based on the relationship they were in, and then—TADA!—found someone else to marry. I truly believe that some people just believe in the business of marriage itself and some don't. That's okay. The right person can definitely trigger all of those feelings and it's not impossible to convert a nonmarrying type into the perfect spouse, but the longevity is something that will require the work. You just have to want it enough for yourself and your other half.

Love Each Other into Your Dreams

Is there a fine line between being overly dependent and healthfully codependent? How do you figure out how to create healthy boundaries in your relationship? Can you be courageous enough to let the other person know when they've crossed the line and it's too much? What does it look like to be a genuine teammate to your partner without being overbearing?

Codependency in a relationship isn't necessarily a bad thing. We have been attached to our love for each other and our ambition for each other's success throughout our relationship. Both of us have always championed each other's dreams and have always been each other's biggest cheerleaders. We've grown to understand that our codependency has been a healthy ingredient for us to lean on each other for support and use each other's perspectives as a healthy checkpoint as we're moving forward in our life's pursuits.

It's important to learn how to function in a healthy marriage as a team without losing yourself in the process.

Devale

I've heard people say that having a codependency on someone else can be detrimental to your own personal mental health. That is true, but I would challenge that assumption in all relationships. Khadeen and I are definitely codependent on each other, but I would say that it's been healthy because neither one of us has ever considered life without the other. Similar to words like *addiction* or *obsessive*, many of the world's most successful people have admitted to having addictive or obsessive relationships with their passions. This obsessive behavior may seem extreme to others but it contributes to what makes them great at what they do. And the truth is, no one else has to understand your obsession as long as it continues to drive you forward in a positive way. Another term that has been used to describe a healthy team environment is interdependency, but I for one am obsessed with the idea of building a great life with Kay. Nothing else is more important to me. I believe that pursuing the same goals and raising our family with those same collective goals has built more trust in our relationship.

If you're truly committed to being with that person for

eternity, and that person is truly committed to you, there is no idea that that person is not going to support without a discussion. I have never thought about what my life would be like without Khadeen and vice versa. That doesn't mean that she's going to do everything I want or everything I need. I have to be willing to give grace and be accepting of who Khadeen is, not only for who she was when we met but who she is today and who she will be tomorrow. When you can learn to love someone unconditionally, that means that you will love them regardless of the choices and decisions they make (within reason, of course). The beauty in this trust is that of a seesaw. Constant movement makes it fun because you know that your partner is putting in the work on the other end to ensure you go up when you need that thrust. You don't have to say "Go!" It just happens.

When you are willing to learn to love unconditionally, you are in a better position to create a life that is beneficial for both you and your partner. Having Khadeen in my corner to give her perspective has helped me to eliminate a lot of blind spots. When I think about Kay, I imagine being in a gunfight with someone who is standing securely at my back. As I'm looking ahead, I can see everything in my peripheral vision, but I can't see anything behind me. I'm not concerned about that because my partner has my back. That is the level of trust that can create a codependency, for sure. But when you've picked the right partner, you can thrive.

One of the things that I feel has helped Khadeen and me

in our relationship is having a plan. We always had our eyes toward a future together. As our goals are now so intertwined, it has made us realize that when other things in our relationship aren't functioning the way we expect them to, we can always come back to the bigger goal. For example, there were times in college where Khadeen and I felt like we didn't want to be together, and we took breaks from our relationship. During those times, we decided whether or not we were going to see other people. For me, no one else brought anything to the table that was equivalent to what Khadeen provided.

When you're young and you're thinking about being with someone, your main focus is sexual attraction and having fun. But we spent the first two weeks of our relationship talking about how we wanted to live as adults and building our dream together. Our dreams became our focus. So when things didn't work out perfectly because we were in a rut, there was no need to run out and find someone else. My goal was never to just have a partner that I wanted to have sex with. When we were going through our phases where we were constantly evolving and changing, I could always look at Khadeen and say, "Despite what's going on right now, we have a plan and a goal together." And not for nothing, sitting down and planning our life together is what kept us together.

Being on the same page about our future is what made me fall in love with her even more because I felt like I had a partner. I've never walked out into the world a day in my life and felt alone simply because I knew I had Khadeen with me. Even if we fucked things up, I knew that we could always go back to the drawing board, set up a new plan, and figure out a new way. There has been no one else in my life that I've been able to sit down and plan my life with. When two people can plan their life and fail, grow, laugh, succeed, and celebrate their goals together, it makes life that much more worth living.

Khadeen

So much of our lives are intertwined, but even in that, there's a duality between being individuals and being in a relationship. There are so many layers to our relationship, where it's just not one thing that attracts us or one thing that I think holds us together. We have mutual respect for each other as partners and lovers, we have discovered how to be good coparents together, and I believe we are great partners in crime in every aspect of our business.

One phase of life that I always say I missed out on was having my own place. I literally went from my parents' home to Devale's house in Michigan when he was playing for the Detroit Lions and we've been living together ever since. Before this, there were our college days where we went from sleeping together on my twin-size bed in my single dorm room to my on-campus apartment. I don't know what it feels like to be out on my own. Sometimes I joke with Devale and say that I kind of want to have my own place. Even now as a married woman with four kids, I sometimes dream about having a one-bedroom apartment in Miami or Los Angeles. In truth, this also might be the Sagittarius in me that likes to be alone and the ability to be able to pick up and go at times. But if I had a choice between the life I live now and a little more independence, I wouldn't have changed a thing.

It's also been a joy for me to see Devale through all the dreams, aspirations, and hopes that he has for himself. It's almost as if I'm sitting with this front-row seat to his life and watching it unfold like a movie. With every disappointment, every yes, every no, and every victory, I experience his dreams along with him. It's like being on the best ride of my life. I admire Devale's drive and persistence, too. Devale is literally out here doing every single thing that he said he wanted to do. I just am in awe of everything that he is accomplishing, all while now being a present father and husband.

While having never lived alone might have hindered me as I was learning to grow as an individual, I think it was also beneficial because I never felt like I was alone in anything. With Devale at my side, I always had somebody rooting for me. When the time came for me to finish up grad school and I was looking to start a career in broadcast journalism, I was looking for small markets to move to. Without hesitation, Devale said, "Come to Michigan with me. We'll have each other and I can support you and you can support me." Of course we wanted to be together, but this gave us a real opportunity to see how we could make things work individually in our careers.

When I went to Michigan, I loved having someone who was always in my corner. Those were some of the benefits in having someone as my partner early on, but it doesn't stop me from wondering how our relationship would have evolved if we had given ourselves more freedom to explore our lives individually before we became a serious couple. When we talk to our single friends, Devale and I sometimes joke with them, "Man, we wish we could have your kind of freedom." And many of them are quick to holla back and say, "I wish I had someone to come home to and some kids to meet me at the door."

At times, I wished we could have experienced other people, other situations, and other scenarios during college. We did try to intentionally spend time apart during part of his first year in the NFL. During the time apart, all we did was crave being together more—and it spiced things up for us when we would reconnect for long weekends in New York or when I went to Detroit for his game. In retrospect, I think it would've benefited us more if we'd had an open mind and really allowed ourselves to explore other things. But we were so booed up that it was almost impossible to try to spend time apart.

KHADEEN'S HOT TAKE
Completing Yourself

Before you get into *any* relationship, you have to be real and ask yourself, "Am I looking for someone to complete me?" For most modern women, we know what we bring to the table. We're confident about our education, our jobs, our businesses, and our possessions. But there is still a part of us that feels like we won't be complete until we find someone else to make us happy. Ladies, if you are looking for someone else to make you whole, you're setting yourself up for failure.

As much as I love Devale, it would be very selfish of me to view my marriage from the vantage point of expecting him to validate my worth and to complete the picture of who I am as a woman. That is my job—not his. Don't get me wrong, it feels good when my husband grabs my butt when I'm walking by or when he affirms my strength after giving birth to our children. But at the end of the day, Khadeen's worth has to be defined and affirmed by Khadeen.

Nobody's expecting you to show up perfectly whole in a relationship—but before you do, make sure that you are good for and with yourself. Be good with spending time alone. Be good with understanding your strengths and your weaknesses. Be good with knowing who you are individually, in a relationship, and in a collective group. Knowing who you are and being confident that you can complete yourself will go a long way in being the kind of partner you want to be and attracting and keeping a partner who will be compatible to your needs.

Devale

During the spring of my sophomore year, I fractured my index finger pretty bad playing ball. I was scheduled for surgery on a Saturday morning and Khadeen had already made provisions to drive me to the hospital for the special surgery in Manhattan. I remember my father meeting us there after the surgery was over, and Kay was taking notes of all the post-op care I would need for the next few days. She drove me back to the dorm and had all my prescriptions filled while I slept.

Three days post-surgery, I remember not feeling so well and the pain in my finger was unbearable. I was taking two Vicodin every four hours as prescribed to dull the shock of having a plate put in my finger, but I didn't have much of an appetite. I'll never forget this day because it was the day Kay came through for me 100 percent. I couldn't sleep the night before because of the pain and I had to be up early to attend spring ball meetings. Kay had class and I didn't eat breakfast, but I made sure to grab those Vikes. After the meetings I had class, and after class I had to go watch practice. After practice I was feeling so tired that I went back to my room and went to sleep.

I remember Kay calling me after her last class and asking me if I was hungry. I was barely coherent and said, "No." She came to my room anyway with a sandwich from the cafeteria. She told me I didn't look good and demanded that I eat. My finger was throbbing so I immediately reached for the Vikes that I had been taking religiously every four hours all day, but Kay grabbed them first and said, "I'm pretty sure you didn't eat all day and you're not taking another pill without putting something in your stomach." I agreed but felt woozy and couldn't even sit up to eat. Kay broke off pieces of the sandwich to feed me, but after three bites I had to rush to the bathroom. I started vomiting up bile and a white foamy substance over and over again. It was the pills I had taken before I went to sleep. Kay stood over me and rubbed my back while giving me water to sip.

She remained just as caring all through college and is still like that today. On my busy days, she will make sure that I carry a lunch with me because she knows I wouldn't stop to eat otherwise. At nights when I come back from practice, training, or filming, she'll sit down and stretch me. She'll run my bath so that I get into a hot tub to make sure my muscles are relaxed. The simple things that I need to do to be a fully functional person, Khadeen has always made sure that I was doing it. To be honest, if I didn't have her to make sure that

I was doing all these necessary things to keep me organized and healthy, I'd probably be all over the place.

Khadeen

When I met Devale, he told me early on that football was a means to an end for him. Looking at him when he was 140 pounds soaking wet, I was like, "Bro, are you really trying to do this football thing?!" When I saw football players on TV, what stuck out the most for me was that these were huge guys and I didn't know how Devale would stack up against them. I knew nothing about the football world nor was I invested in it at all. But seeing how driven and determined he was, that was enough for me to want to support him through it. I really admired him for being so focused on football in college and strategizing about how he would use his time on the field to set himself up for the rest of his life and to really pursue his true love of acting.

His time in Detroit was truly a sacrificial period for him and I wanted to make sure that I was supporting him. I remember telling him at the time, "If this is what you have to do, I'm going to help you do it." I always made sure that he was eating and that he was taken care of. I genuinely wanted to see him do well and succeed.

For me, it was super easy to support him through his surgeries. Even just the move to Detroit was something that I knew would help him. It was in a low-key way going to help me, too, because I had missed him so much at that time. I knew it was just going to be better for him if I was there. I was willing to sacrifice a little bit of time from getting my career started to be there for him in whatever capacity he needed me. At that time, I focused on being present whenever he was home, making good meals, being good company, and hanging out during his downtime.

When he had challenges with prescription drugs during his time in the NFL, I knew something was off and that something was bothering him. I didn't know the extent of it until he told me that he was taking his medication just to function. At the time, it made me feel like I was dealing with someone who had PTSD. He was in a bad place and I could tell that we weren't connecting on the level that I was used to. Once I realized what was happening, I tried my hardest to figure out the best way to help him. He shut me out to an extent because he didn't think he had a problem.

Looking back now, I remember that he was always trying to pick fights with me. He would be upset when I was home in New York and hanging out with my friends just trying to pass the time. He thought that I was using that time to move forward from our relationship. I remember him saying to me several times, "If I'm going to be at home in Detroit in my room at night missing you, you should be doing the same thing in New York. You shouldn't be out with your friends, having a good time. You should be in your house." To me, it felt like he was being incredibly selfish and inconsiderate of how I was feeling during this time in our relationship.

But regardless of all that, I still wanted us to be in a good place and to keep our relationship healthy and strong. Fortunately, we were able to work things out, particularly when he told his coach about his challenges with the pain medication. Things started to make a lot more sense and I was able to give him a little bit more grace in that circumstance to understand. I didn't think it would've been in his best interest either for me to walk away at that point or for me to step back. If anything, I needed to lean into him more to be a support system for him. That's why it was super important for me to just be there.

We had a lot of people who were not necessarily rooting for us to fail, but they were giving us what they thought was a fair warning. Particularly when Devale went to the NFL, he heard the same thing over and over: "Why would you want to have a girlfriend and be bogged down with just one person when you're going to have women at your disposal?" Then there were people in my ear saying, "Girl, now's your time. While he's away, you can be doing your thing."

Devale and I had many moments where we were seriously discussing not being together because we were trying to take heed to what people were saying. In those early days, we would find ourselves saying to each other, "Maybe they're right, maybe this won't last. Maybe we should be out there, exploring and meeting other people." It's almost like we were trying to make sure that there was no stone unturned before deciding to commit fully to each other. But every single time that we tried not to be together, I think it pulled us closer together. Maybe I can blame that on our codependency, but here we are, twenty years later, thinking about how we still continue to live, love, laugh, and be together. I could not envision my life without Devale now, nor could I have then.

Devale

When it came time to help Khadeen with her dream to become a traffic reporter after college, if I'm being honest, I was so supportive because I wanted to prove her mom wrong. Yeah, my level of petty is Hall of Fame–worthy. At the beginning of our relationship, I knew she was afraid that I was going to love her daughter into failure and become a distraction. She never minced words when it came to her disapproval of our codependency—although she never called it that, and at the time, we didn't see it that way. She made it very clear to Kay that "I was going to ruin her life."

Yes, I said *"ruin her life"*! She said that to me verbatim one night after a failed attempt by Kay to correct an issue with a phone bill. The summer of 2003, Kay went away with her family to Jamaica for ten days. This was the longest we had ever been away from each other at that time. We spoke for hours every day, not knowing that her phone was roaming. At the end of the month, her brother called her at school and asked what was up with the nine-hundred-dollar phone bill. Kay tried to get ahead of it by calling AT&T, but they needed her father to verify his Social Security number, so she asked me to say that I was Morrison Joseph and to get access to the account. I did it. I'm not sure how, but her mom found out and immediately called Kay spazzing. She then told Kay to put me on the phone. Kay looked at me and I gestured for her to hand it over. Kay's mom proceeded to blame me for the whole thing and told me that she was not going to let my actions ruin Kay's life. I ended the conversation by saying that I love Khadeen and would never do anything to jeopardize her future. I hung up and then told Kay I was never going by her parents' house again. That was the beginning of the two-year hiatus. Now as a parent, I can understand my mother-in-law's fear. Being the young, fierce competitor that I was then (and continue to be!), I wanted to prove her wrong so badly.

At first, I just saw Khadeen as my partner to help me achieve my goals. But as I saw her start to ascend in her own dreams, my thought process changed. I said, "Wait a minute. There can be more than one star here." I was now just as committed to her happiness and success as I was for myself. My motivation for helping Khadeen evolved from wanting to prove her mom wrong to wanting to see her be happy. I wanted to see her have a level of success that I had reached making it in the NFL, because I knew that she worked so hard.

As a man, you have these dreams and ideals of what you want to do to be the breadwinner for your family. But you rarely get a chance to watch a woman have the same dreams because we've been conditioned to feel that men are supposed to be the breadwinner and women are supposed to be the person behind the great man. But in the moment where she started to ascend, I became proud of being the man behind the great woman. I wanted this dream so much for her because I wanted her to be able to raise her hand and say "Yes, I did this for me."

Watching Khadeen rise and become better at her craft definitely became an addiction for me. It got to a point where I wanted Khadeen to be successful more than I think Khadeen wanted to be successful for herself. Once again, that's the competitive edge in me. I wanted Khadeen to win everything. Khadeen was a pageant girl, and I knew how hard she worked and pushed herself to be great in that arena. I wanted her to have that same success as a traffic reporter. She ultimately made it to the top five in that competition before the news station decided to go in another direction. But even though she didn't get the position, it was the beginning of so many great skills that she cultivated over time and that has made her a great podcaster and social media influencer.

Ironically, as competitive as I am, I find pleasure in watching other people be happy and find their purpose in life. I watched my father mentor young men into making better decisions. I watched my mom work within her community to be of service to people and make people happy. I believe seeing my parents in that kind of selfless service became part of who I became as a man and ultimately as a husband and partner to Khadeen. When it came to having a partner, as much as I wanted to be great, I didn't want a partner that's behind me. I want to watch my partner walk in her purpose and find her own happiness so that we can create happiness together. I am deeply committed to creating a life of abundance with Khadeen so that we can be of service to other people.

I don't think it's possible to have happiness in a relationship if one person is dependent on watching the other person become great. What if your partner doesn't succeed? Now what does your partner or spouse have for themselves? It was the duality of chasing my own greatness while also pushing Khadeen to be great that helped us succeed together. Watching her chase her own greatness while she was pushing me to be great is what really makes us click as a couple. Nothing is more important to either one of us than watching the other one be happy and feel fulfilled with what they're doing in life. And, look, you don't need to be as driven as we are in order to be fulfilled in your relationship—but working toward a common goal (or two complementary goals) is a fantastic way to enhance your bond and learn how to function as a team.

Chapter Seven

There's a Marriage After This Wedding (Or, When the Real Work Begins)

One of the biggest things that we learned in the process of planning our wedding is that we had completely different priorities. While Devale was focused on making sure we were financially secure after our wedding, Khadeen wanted to have the biggest and baddest wedding that anyone had ever seen. This clash of priorities made for a rough road during our first year of marriage. That road became even rockier when, unbeknownst to us, we would be expecting our first child just a year after we said "I do." It took us quite some time to get on the same page about what it meant to build a stable foundation for our family, find a solid financial footing, and respect each other's different points of view.

Life has a way of shifting your priorities in your marriage, whether it's starting your marriage with a blended family, caring for aging parents, weathering the storm of unexpected financial challenges, or just dealing with the unending ebbs and flows of life. Who gets to say what the priorities are in the moment? How do you pivot without losing the foundation of your relationship? When is it time to ask for outside support from a spiritual adviser or a mental health professional? Discovering what your priorities are and having the courage to reprioritize as needed is a learning and growing process in every relationship. In this chapter, we will break down what it means to prioritize your values and goals in your relationship and how to make sure that you maintain the love and commitment to each other without losing yourself throughout the journey.

Devale

Going into 2008, I was slated to be the starting kick returner and the number three receiver. Everything was going as planned. I had my fiancée and now I was focused on giving her the wedding of her dreams. Seemingly everyone around me was planning these platinum, over-the-top weddings with six-figure budgets. Being a professional athlete and having two friends in the NFL who were married during the same time, I knew I would have to do the same. That's where a large part of the pressure was coming from. My focus was to put myself in a position financially to not only give my fiancée the wedding that she deserved, but to also be able to give her the life we planned after that wedding. I still wanted us to continue to chase our dreams.

That was important to me because I've always been aware of economic issues. Being a Black man in America, I realized how different our course to getting married was as opposed to our white counterparts. I had white buddies in college who were able to graduate debt free because their parents were able to set them up with generational wealth. Khadeen and I didn't have that. Those same white counterparts were able to walk into their family's business or sit on the board of their family's company. So they walked out of college without debt and then into a job paying upward of eighty thousand dollars per year.

When I got married, I knew that I had to pay for all of it by myself. I knew that my parents did not have the funds to give me a down payment for a home. I knew that Kay's parents couldn't pay for our wedding. After I proposed, I knew that I had to have money in the bank to be able to provide this type of lifestyle for my wife. I wanted my wife to have everything that I saw every other woman had. That was me buying into the American dream. As a protector and a provider, I was making sure not only that I gave her the wedding but that I could provide her with a comfortable lifestyle after that. My goal was to be financially prepared to give us autonomy over our life after we got married, not just on our wedding day. At this point I had more than two hundred thousand dollars in the bank and I was scheduled to make a half a million by the end of the season. I planned that by the end of the year, I'd have about four hundred thousand in my bank account after taxes and paying my agents. I figured we could plan a dope wedding and start a good life with that money.

Then everything fell apart. In 2008, I was expected to make the football team, but I got cut. Then the country was on the cusp of the biggest recession that the world had ever seen since the Great Depression. Every day I was losing anywhere between four thousand to five thousand dollars because the market was rapidly plummeting. By the time September started, my account had dwindled. I spoke to my financial adviser and said, "Bro, I have to take this money out of the stock market because I need cash to survive till the end of the year." He was like, "If you take this money out, you're never going to get it back."

I had no other choice. I was the only one in my family who was able to provide for anything. I ended up taking my money out of the stock market and liquefying those assets in order to be able to survive until the next season started. I wasn't thinking about a wedding anymore. I was thinking about surviving.

Khadeen

I was stupid to think that a wedding would've solved our prior issues with each other or would've expunged the history that we had. There were certain things that naturally transitioned into marriage because so much of the fabric of who we were as people was already woven into our entire relationship. But once we were engaged, Devale said, "We don't have to get married right away. I just wanted to show you that I'm committed to you and that I'm serious. We can be engaged for a couple years and eventually plan a wedding a few years down the road." That hit me like a ton of bricks because I'm like "Wait a second. I never said I wanted a long engagement!" I envisioned that we would be married within two years at the most.

I felt like he had just proposed to shut me up. The last thing I wanted was another nine years of chilling in limbo. This was yet another moment in time where Devale had his idea of what he thought he was doing and I had my own idea of where I thought we were headed. We were not on the same page.

We decided to proceed with the wedding at the time because I believed that Devale was trying to appease me. At this point, he was just so tired of the back-and-forth with the politics of the NFL that he no longer wanted them to dictate his livelihood. He wanted to take control of his livelihood. I didn't think it was a smart decision at the time. So when he mentioned to me that he was thinking about potentially retiring and I would need to choose between a wedding and a house, I said, "If we don't have a home right now, I'm okay with that. Let's have the wedding. After the wedding we can find a house and live wherever we want to live." Low-key, my spoiled ass was, like, "We gonna get both!"

We headed back to Brooklyn, where gentrification and the recession were hitting all at once. We would've been able to get a brownstone in Brooklyn for dirt cheap, but unfortunately we did not have the foresight to see the housing market at the time. I was solely focused on our wedding. I figured we could have the wedding and get the house a year later. Why not celebrate the moment? After all, it was one day that we could never get back.

I was also willing to work and pull my weight, too. It was a no-brainer to me, but things didn't quite pan out that way. We ended up having the wedding with 330 guests. We had a lot of people who were excited about our union and we both felt a little bit of pressure to make everyone happy. We were one of the first couples of our generation to get married, so everyone wanted to be involved. I am the first grandchild on my mom's side, the first niece and oldest cousin, so the family's excitement was in abundance. I really wanted a destination wedding, but between my paternal grandmother, who was my literal best friend, being ill and Devale's grandfather refusing to fly ever, we were not willing to forfeit their presence. That's when I knew this was going to be a big-ass wedding. And that it was. Looking back on it, of course, it was a poor investment. Did we have a great time? We sure did! But while we were planning the wedding, we were definitely at odds over how to proceed. Ultimately, Devale was trying to give me what I wanted. When I look back now, I can see that it was selfish of me because I wasn't seeing the total picture of things. I can understand now why Devale was more concerned about making sure we would be able to live comfortably after the wedding.

Devale

Before we started planning the wedding, I was practically living paycheck to paycheck the entire fall of 2008 and trying to figure out how I was going to recoup all of the things that I had lost. All of the property that I had bought in 2007 had now depreciated because the housing bubble had burst. I was pretty much upside down on those mortgages.

At this point, I was extremely depressed. Kay didn't want to be in Michigan away from her family. I was working as a learning coordinator for the University of Michigan men's basketball team that fall. I wanted to stay in Michigan because we had a home there and I had a community of support because I played for the Lions, but Kay wanted to be closer to her family. We moved back to my grandparents' apartment in Brooklyn in January 2009. I got signed by the Cleveland Browns in December 2008. Two weeks after I signed with them, they fired their head coach Romeo Crennel. I went from being one of the guys that they were looking at, at the top of the roster, to being at the bottom of the roster again.

I didn't want to do this all over again. During all of 2009, Khadeen was excited about being engaged. Meanwhile, I was trying to focus on how to get all these bills paid. I never let Khadeen know how bad it was. My dad always told me that as a protector and a provider, "You never let your wife know how bad things are. We as men have to figure that out."

In the meantime, my brother and I started to build a business together. We pooled our resources to make sure we could make it through as a family. Fortunately, I was able to relax a little bit because we were living in a rent-stabilized apartment and splitting the rent with my brother and another couple who had rented the apartment while we were in Michigan.

When I got back to Cleveland, I realized I wasn't going to make this team. The new coach, Eric Mangini, brought in all his former players from the Jets. I knew for a fact that I was not going to make the team because he was giving everyone else those opportunities.

I knew it wasn't anything personal, it's just business in football. When you're starting a new team, you go with the people you know. I got a phone call from the front office in late August with an Ohio area code. I knew they were calling me because they had to sign draft picks and let some people go. Sure enough, by the end of the day, my NFL career was done.

That same day Khadeen says to me, "We have a venue appointment at Oheka Castle." I wasn't thinking about no wedding. I almost lost it.

In 2009, the per head price for Oheka Castle was $325 per plate. Our guest list was more than two hundred and fifty people. That meant that would be at least $80,000 just for the venue. When we get back to our parents' house and we're sitting on the couch, I say, "If I'm being honest, I think we need to hold off on the wedding."

"What do you mean?"

"I just want to figure out where things are going to be with our finances."

"Well, I don't want to be engaged for too long."

"You have a choice. We could buy a home. If we buy the home, the money I was going to put toward the wedding is going to have to be a down payment. Or we can get married right away and have the wedding you want, but we would still have to live in the apartment for a couple of years."

Without hesitation, Khadeen says, "I choose the wedding. I don't mind living in the apartment."

Ultimately, I just wanted to see my wife smile and be happy. If I could do it all over again, I wouldn't even ask her. I could have put that fifty thousand dollars as a down payment because they were selling brownstones around the corner from us for a quarter mil. Our mortgage would've been probably eighteen hundred a month. And we would've found a way to make it work. But no, I wanted to see my wife smile. I wanted to feel like a man, because I gave my wife the wedding that she wanted. And ultimately, that was a stupid idea.

DEVALE'S HOT TAKE

The Pressure to Get to the Ring

When Khadeen gave me her standards for the next step in
our relationship, it created pressure for me. I also felt pressure from being in the NFL at that time to give Khadeen
the same kind of big wedding that my teammates were
giving their wives. I'll admit that my ego made me want to
prove to everybody else that I was successful enough to
deliver these things for my future wife.

The idea of marriage itself did not scare me as much
as providing the type of wedding and then the financial
security for the rest of my life with Khadeen. Back then, I
didn't know a lot of things about the day-to-day work on
making the decision to be committed to Khadeen every
day. Either I could rise to the pressure or I could say no. But
I chose to rise to that moment and make the next chapter
for us—our engagement and our marriage—happen.

Ultimately, marrying Khadeen was the best decision
I've ever made because it showed me that I can make
things happen even when it's not on my timeline. I learned
through our marriage that how you get married and the
decisions you make leading up to getting to the altar will
define the first few years of your marriage.

Taking the next step in your relationship—whether it's

declaring exclusivity, an engagement, a marriage, or beginning your family—requires that you give yourself the time to be serious, thoughtful, and forward-thinking about the kind of future you want to create. Although Khadeen's pressure worked out for me, you should make sure that you don't let one person's pressure push you faster than you are ready to do so. Additionally, *gentlemen*, recognize when you are putting pressure on yourself and creating unrealistic expectations fueled by your own ego. If the pressure in your relationship isn't pushing you toward becoming a diamond, let that coal stay in the mine until it's ready to shine.

Khadeen

I was just one of those girls who always dreamed about their wedding day. I never quite knew what my groom was going to look like. However, I was enamored by all things wedding. As a former pageant girl, I was big into the glitz and the glam of the event. Now that I was finally engaged to the man of my dreams, I was totally looking forward to planning a beautiful wedding.

It's crazy because when I look at it now, as desperate as I was to become a wife, I was not prepared to be one. However, there was no conversation with my mom or any other woman in my family who really sat me down and said,

"Khadeen, here's what it takes to be a wife." I can appreciate that no one really told me anything because I feel like the advice would've come from women who were already tainted or jaded by their own relationships. I'm not sure how sound the advice would've been because everyone's relationship is different. Everyone's complaints were different. And to be honest, I hadn't been privy to or witnessed happy, successful marriages around me. I didn't necessarily want the advice, nor was I yearning for the advice from any women in my life, except for, maybe, one of my aunts. She appeared to be in a genuine, happy relationship, but you never really know what's happening in someone else's relationship. There simply weren't many people that I could look up to and say, "Wow, I would love to model my relationship after theirs." Hashtag relationship goals were nowhere to be found, and I was going to have to figure out this wife thing on my own, hoping that it wouldn't be to the detriment of my marriage.

As much as Devale wants to say that I was pressuring him into an engagement in my mind, it was time. We had been dating for about seven years. For me, it was a matter of wondering what was next. Did I ever have any doubts that Devale would want to be with me for the rest of my life? No, but I was very wrapped up in this timeline that I had in my mind of where I should be at a particular point in my life.

Because we started dating at a young age, there was so much that transpired during the course of our relationship for those four years between meeting each other and the turmoil that happened within his first year in the NFL and my first grad-school year. Those moments made me feel like our relationship could really stand the test of time. It felt like it was time and marriage was simply the next natural step.

Not to mention when you're younger, you tend to see what other couples are doing and start to compare. We were hanging around a lot of people within the league as well as people who we knew from college who were already married, engaged, or at least had one child at that point. It's funny how just being in the midst of that can totally skew how you see your life and how you gauge the trajectory of success. I had always told myself, "I want to be married and have all my kids before thirty." Ha! Joke was on me. In my mind, I felt like there was this clock counting down the time between each of the goals I wanted to achieve. It wasn't my biological clock, per se, but there was the clock silently saying "Khadeen, you should be here at this point in your life. You should be there. You should have accomplished this. You should have done that."

I felt like once Devale proposed to me, we could get a wedding in motion, be married, and start making serious decisions toward starting a family. Little did I know that in his mind, a proposal would just be a promise to marry at some point, just not right away. I also never anticipated Devale wanting to retire from the NFL in that time frame either. He just had some more left to do in the league, or at least that was my opinion. I'd witnessed him make the Detroit Lions as a free agent walk-on and he had barely scratched the surface of his potential in the NFL. Unfortunately, I wasn't the one calling the shots and he, too, had little to no control over his fate. I knew and was confident that he was on top of things when it came to finances and making proper investments, especially after he got into the league. So I felt like as long as he had these NFL new opportunities, then our financial stability wouldn't be a problem.

But it was the imperfect storm of events that started to happen once we began talking seriously about being engaged. With all the certainty I had in wanting to be Devale's wife, he was met with career uncertainty in the league. I was so wrapped up in officially starting our forever that I could not even see the dimmed light in his eyes. I couldn't recognize that he was battling with the unknown about his future, all while actively thinking about our future. I think back to a conversation he and I had over dinner at our favorite restaurant in Dearborn, Michigan, at the time, Big Fish. The catalyst for this talk—me changing my screen saver on my laptop to a photo of my "dream ring." A bit forward and pretentious? Maybe. Or maybe I was manifesting our nuptials (yes, I was doing it before the word *manifesting* became mainstream). Devale flat-out told me, "Every man has a plan when it comes to the proposal and marriage. A man has the pressure of planning, saving, selecting, and preparing, and essentially, no one deserves the right to rush his process." I did not even think about the process from his perspective, and the more we talked about it, the more I respected him for wanting to make sure that he would be able to care for me in the capacity he wanted to as a future husband. I honestly was not thinking about life after the proposal or the wedding because I was so confident that everything would work out. Instead, Devale, being a bit of a traditional man, knew that he wanted to be able to provide me with a life of ease, stability, and abundance. How could I be upset at that? Still, wallowing in selfishness and immaturity, all I knew was that I was heading into my late twenties and wanted to think about having kids as soon as possible and for damn sure wasn't about to be somebody's baby mama.

These were the things that made me feel like I had to be adamant with Devale about where we were going next. I needed clarity. I knew he was focusing on purchasing a house in Michigan and that he was serious about creating a solid future for us. In my mind, I was like, "I didn't ask you for a house!" Not that I didn't appreciate him thinking forward for us; however, a house was not something that I said I necessarily wanted in that moment. This was mainly because I didn't know if I saw a future for us in Michigan and never really enjoyed being so far away from family and friends. He was making a financial move into ownership and making a palpable investment in our future. Devale always spoke about not wanting to rent and having his own property. When he purchased the home, I thought that was a sound financial move he was making and not necessarily something he was purchasing for me. I was such a planner at that time. I needed to know my one-year, three-year, and five-year plans. I didn't want to be the girl who was traveling after a man and just following him from state to state, with my career in limbo, and not knowing what we were going to be doing next in terms of our relationship. I didn't want to be his shadow. I could clearly hear my mom's voice in my ear telling me that no matter what, I needed to have my own. I got it. No mom wants to see her child dependent on another person. She also instilled the mindset in me that I needed to be a contributing member of a relationship and household. My parents made sacrifice after sacrifice to ensure that I had everything I needed and, in most cases, everything I wanted. My mom believed so much in my ability that I now can understand her fear and apprehension around me living with my boyfriend out of state with no stable career. Man, that convo I had to have with her and my dad when I decided I wanted to make the move to Michigan. Bruhhh! I practiced over and over again what I would say, how I would say it, and when the right time would be. I know my mom already felt like Devale had just swooped in and taken over. I always had anxiety when it came to talking to my parents, particularly if I knew it might be met with disdain.

The proposal happened during Devale's brother's graduation party. It wasn't uncommon for his family to have a get-together or barbecue. My family was also at the event, which happened often because our families jelled together well. If

Devale wanted his intentions to go unnoticed, it was best for him to do it at an event like that because I would've never expected it. To my knowledge, Devale didn't tell any of the women in the family—except for asking my mom for her blessing, of course, before he proposed.

I was surprised, because Devale was very low-key that entire day. He didn't give me any inclination or any feeling that he was a little nervous, apprehensive, or anxious about the whole proposal. He was really keeping it on the down low. There were at least sixty of our closest friends and family all gathered in the backyard.

Devale goes up to say a couple of words to his brother. He is up on the balcony and everyone is below in the backyard. He starts to talk about his brother, exclaiming how proud he is and what a milestone it is for him to graduate from college. Then he proceeds to talk about how his brother is so amazing and so selfless that he allowed him to share a special moment on his special day. At that time, I always had a camera in my hand. I loved documenting special moments. I was actually taking a video of Devale giving the speech to his brother.

Then I hear the song "Incomplete" by Sisqó playing in the background. I thought it was weird that that song would be playing during his brother's graduation party. I thought somebody mistakenly turned on the radio. But then Devale shifts his focus to me and talks about how much he loves me and how he can't wait to spend the rest of his life with me. I was in such a shock that I could barely focus on what he was saying.

His cousin Porsha grabbed the camera out of my hand so that I could focus on the moment. I looked over at my mom and she was in tears. The crowd that I was standing in parted like the Red Sea and it was just a circle of family and friends around me. I was in the center and Devale came down off the staircase that he was on and got down on his knee and he proposed. Of course I said "Yes" and everyone was in tears at this point. It became a celebration, not just for his brother but for us. It was beautiful because all our family and friends were there to experience that moment with us.

I remember still being on a high toward the end of the night. Then my mom comes over to me with an overnight duffel bag and she says, "I packed a couple of things for you that you're going to need for tonight." Then I was called to the front yard. When I got to the front of the house, there was a limousine, a driver holding flowers and balloons, and Devale standing there with a huge smile. He said, "We're going to the city for the night. I know that it meant a lot for you to have our family and friends close by for the actual proposal. But I also wanted us to have some private alone time to really enjoy the night." He had made arrangements for us to stay in a suite at the Grand Hyatt in the city. When we went to check in, they congratulated us on our engagement. We went up to the room for the night and had a really nice, intimate night together.

The last thing my mom said to me after she helped me get into the limousine was "I'm so happy for you, but please don't get pregnant tonight because we have a wedding to plan." I almost fell out from laughing so hard. That's probably the realest thing my mother ever said to me about sex.

I love that Devale took into consideration having a public moment with our family but also having private time with the two of us to really just celebrate and bask in that moment. After all, I had been waiting for this for a long time.

And it was such a memorable time for us, definitely one of the best days of my life. And I will always remember that Memorial Day weekend that we spent in New York back home in Brooklyn with our family when we got engaged.

KHADEEN'S HOT TAKE
The Pressure to Get to the Ring

I am woman enough to admit now that being around other couples who were engaged or getting married when I was in my late twenties made me more eager to move forward in my own relationship. When Devale and I were considering getting married, we had already been together for six years and it seemed like a natural succession for us.

Was it immature to push Devale toward a wedding without thinking about the marriage? I can say now—
absolutely. I was so focused on having this big, beautiful

wedding day and creating my happily ever after. But what exactly is happy ever after and how do you get there? You cannot measure your life and your relationship against what you see on social media—especially when you're in your twenties.

It's critical to take your time to figure out and learn what your definition of happiness is in your relationship. It could be a long-term committed relationship with just the two of you or a marriage with a bunch of kids like me and Devale. But whatever *your* definition is, make sure that your definition of happily ever after belongs to *you.*

Devale

In May 2008, I decided to propose. I did want to show Khadeen that I wanted to be in it for the long haul. I was also at this point in my life where I was trying to check boxes. Honestly, this was probably the first mistake I made. I was comparing my life and where I was in my twenties to everyone else. Ultimately, I drank the Kool-Aid. The pressure I got was not only from Khadeen but also the pressure I put on myself to prove to everybody that I was successful.

But if I'm being honest, I wasn't ready. I didn't even know what it was like to be married. My father never talked to me about controlling my emotions as a man. We never even had the sex talk. I wasn't prepared to have a wife, let alone plan the rest of my life with someone else. But I did it because I felt that it was just the next logical step.

I'll never forget the day that I proposed. I made a conscious effort to tell all the guys first, and not the women, because I didn't want it to get back to Khadeen that I was thinking about proposing. I told all the men in my family that I was planning on proposing during my brother's college graduation party on Memorial Day weekend.

I remember getting the ring that Khadeen wanted. It was a one-and-a-half-carat white diamond. The ring included a heart with the letters K and D on each side to signify our union. I was glad that it was designed by our jeweler in Michigan, Avie, right before he passed.

The weather was perfect that day and my parents' backyard was filled with family and friends from both sides. During the eight years Kay and I were together, our families became very close. I asked my brother, Brian, if it was okay to propose at his college graduation party. Of course he was fine with it. I did it this way on purpose so that Khadeen would have no idea everyone was there for a proposal. I started by asking everyone to gather around the steps, and I began to make a toast about Brian.

Midway through the toast I transitioned to talking about friendships and soulmates, while Brian hit the CD player and started playing "Incomplete" by Sisqó over the speaker. At this point everyone, who had no idea what was going on, started to look at me weirdly because this grown-ass professional football player was standing on the steps making a speech about his brother with Sisqó playing in the background. Talk about awkward. But then it clicked, and everyone stopped looking at me funny and started staring at Kay, who was holding a camera. My cousin Porsha ran over and snatched the camera from Kay's face. Khadeen looked around and realized that everyone was staring at her. Then she looked up and finally realized what song was playing.

I said, "Khadeen, will you marry me?" She just looked at me and started crying. I ran down the stairs and I got on my knee and she said, "Yes, Devale, I will marry you." I picked her up and I had a car service prepared for us. I had a hotel room planned in the city and we spent the rest of the night there, loving on each other.

Right after the proposal, I felt a moment of accomplishment. But then I started thinking, "What's the next step in being a husband?"

Chapter Eight

Choosing Service Over Selfishness

As we've said, we hate the term "couple goals." It's unfair to your partner to tailor your relationship to someone else's idea of what a relationship should be. Your focus for your relationship should be about being the best version of yourself for your partner. We always want to empower couples to focus on being of service to their partners. The goal here is to not be idolized by other people but to wake up every day trying to be of service to the person that you *chose* to dedicate your life to in partnership. It wasn't until we became pregnant with our second son, Kairo, that we realized that being of service to each other was of paramount importance, not only for our pregnancy but for our marriage.

One of the hardest points in our first few years of marriage was understanding that we couldn't tailor our marriage to anyone else's expectations. We realized that all the things that we thought we wanted out of marriage were all based on social conditioning. We tried to emulate those things and it didn't take long for us to realize that we didn't want any of the things that were presented to us as a happy marriage. For example, we thought we were supposed to follow a script where Devale was just there to be a provider, go to work, and come home, while Khadeen was supposed to cook, clean, have babies, and take care of the home.

We discovered that our happiness came from supporting each other's dreams and goals. Instead of projecting other people's ideals on to each other, we recognized that we both enjoyed being emotionally and physically present for our sons, attending their practices, and making breakfast for them in the morning. Our happiness wasn't tied up in either one of us fulfilling a specific role, but we had to rearrange our mindsets to focus on what worked for us.

In this chapter, we will focus on the act of choosing to be of service in your marriage. We have learned that choosing to be of service to someone for the rest of your life is an unconditional act. You have to be of service to that person, regardless of how they act or behave. You can't choose marriage based on religion, physical appearance, sex, or financial situation. You can only choose a person to marry based on their willingness to be of service as a partner and your willingness to serve. Everything will not fall into place if both of you are not willing to be of service to each other.

Khadeen

There were a lot of difficult points within the first few years because we went through so many transitionary periods. We were transitioning into being husband and wife, becoming parents, and taking on new career paths. We were also subscribing to what we thought a husband and wife should be and what we thought marriage was going to be like. Devale and I bought into these ideas without fully having a conversation about what was truly important for us. The greatest lesson that we learned during this time is that we couldn't make our marriage conform to someone else's idea of what marriage is or what the media and society teaches us that marriage should be. We knew we were going to have adversity and periods of sacrifice, but if we'd been clearer with each other about our expectations and not felt embarrassed to say what we needed, it would've saved us a lot of heartache in the first couple of years.

Devale and I began to have very open conversations about what we wanted from each other, what we wanted out of a marriage, and what we wanted out of life. We talked about what would happen if we divorced, how we would co-parent, and how we could live together under the same roof as an unmarried couple. We got real about our struggles with intimacy and sex as I was dealing with postpartum depression and exhaustion from work. After we had these very honest conversations, that's when things started to take a turn for the better for us. We were slowly but surely getting to a point where we could look at each other and say, "I may not agree with you on this, but I understand where you are coming from" or "I'm willing to compromise with you on that issue."

Devale

I used to base all of my ideas about marriage on the things that I had seen. But after being with Khadeen for twenty years, I realized that I watched a lot of unhealthy, misaligned marriages. I thought marriage was supposed to be miserable and that men were supposed to complain about their wives and that wives were supposed to complain about their husbands. I seriously thought all of that was just par for the course and you had to choose to deal with that if you wanted to raise productive children. It wasn't until I decided that I did not want to be miserable in my marriage and started focusing on communicating my own wants that I began to find peace within my marriage.

Regardless of how hard the pivot might be, it's still my choice to work through it. Once I've decided that I want to continuously work through the pivots, the changes in my marriage have never been detriments to my happiness. In fact, it opened up a whole new world for me actually getting what I always desired. When I've opened up to Khadeen about my ideas of what I wanted and what I needed, she could either make a choice of whether she wanted to be a part of it or not. Every day she chooses to be a part of it. I've watched Kay make consistent efforts to be all that I ask simply because I expressed how important they were to me. Before this, I was under the impression that a man should just do what his wife wants and find happiness in his own vices—because "that's what men do." Don't "nag" her because vulnerability is a female trait. Just shut up and find your peace elsewhere. Those ideals weren't good enough for me. So I choose to talk to Kay about everything, and our marriage has been totally different ever since. We can wake up and smile at each other, regardless of whether or not we're always aligned on the same page because we both know the other is choosing to do the work.

Khadeen

After our wedding, things got real really quickly for us. As we came down from the glitz, glam, and high of the wedding, we were on the honeymoon. My grandmother gifted us with a beautiful trip to Jamaica. Unbeknownst to us, we left the States as two and we were coming back home as a soon-to-be family of three. I had stopped birth control in May, and we figured we would "see what happens." We both knew we were ready to become parents, but we were unsure how long it would take to actually become pregnant. Some couples try for a while, while others barely brush pass each other in the hallway and BOOM! Baby! We were the latter case.

Secrets Wild Orchid in Jamaica had recently opened, and it was the perfect place to unwind, disconnect, and reconnect with each other after the wedding. Our days were filled with sun, sea, and rum, our nights with ganja, dancing, and sweet lovemaking. We met two couples at the resort; one couple was also celebrating their honeymoon and the other couple was enjoying a birthday trip. We kept in touch via Facebook after the trip because both couples were dope and we really enjoyed each other's company while abroad. The other honeymooning couple messaged me a little over a month after the trip to let us know they were expecting. A few days later the birthday couple popped up in our inbox with a "Baby on Board" message. I remember saying, "Oh, shit! Devale, both of the couples are pregnant." He laughed and was like "Yo! That's wild!" Our laughter and disbelief slowly turned into looks of "Oh, shit, what if . . ." My period, which was due any day, never came. I was expecting our first baby, along with our Jamaica-trip buddies. We were all due within days of one another. The other women ended up having a son and a daughter on the same day and I delivered two weeks after them. It was safe to say Jamaica owed us not a damn thing and our lives were forever changed in the best way possible when we welcomed our sweet Jackson into the world that April.

Our focus immediately shifted to becoming parents. We were excited that we had conceived our first child shortly after our wedding and we felt like we were prepared to be good parents. I always desired children and a spouse. Meeting and falling in love with Devale over the years only heightened this craving for me. Maybe it's because we both wanted to have our own family and I saw so much potential in Devale being an amazing father. I always said to myself, "If he approached fatherhood with the intensity that he did everything else in his life, he'd be second to none."

In my timeline, becoming a mother seemed like the natural succession of events for us after the wedding and I was thrilled it happened when it did. While we were looking forward to putting all our energy and our investment into being the best parents that we could be for our son, our roles as husband and wife fell by the wayside. Knowing Devale, I'm certain that his mind was focused on this new responsibility of becoming a father, continuing to take care of his wife, and ensuring that he was doing everything in his power to provide for our growing family. Devale always talked about his father's instruction to him that a wife's income should be supplemental to the family and that as the man he should always be the primary breadwinner.

As we prepared for our first son, Devale had a lot on his plate. He was transitioning out of the NFL and he wanted to start a business as an athletic training company for young people in Brooklyn. We were both in for a rude awakening because his post-NFL dreams weren't going to happen overnight, and we didn't have money coming in like we were accustomed to. If starting from scratch was a couple, that would be us. We lost a ton of money during the recession in the stock market, even after making well-thought-out investments and not spending frivolously. But still, rock bottom was our new dwelling.

My emphasis now was on doing my part to pick up the slack. Even going back to our college days, when his meal-card money would run low, I would pitch in with my money from my stipend to make sure we had enough groceries or that we could go out for a little meal. The Pick 3 menu at Friday's came through in the clutch in those budgeted date nights that we were so fond of. That would leave us with just enough money to head to the Blockbuster video store on the way back to rent a VHS and grab some gummy worms for movie night. My mentality was, I had him and he had me. There was never a reason to panic because we held each other down. We were always going to be working together to make our dreams happen and that was a nonnegotiable.

During that time when it seemed like our money was just sliding out of our hands, I got my ass up and went to look for work. The recession killed any chances of me finding a decent job in news or entertainment. As a first-time mom, I felt like I was the only one equipped enough to care for my baby. I really wasn't ready to leave Jackson so soon. But we needed health insurance and we did not want to be irresponsible with a child. There was conflict within Devale as I prepared to go to MAC in New York. He encouraged me because we both understood that I needed this job, but he, being prideful, was uneasy about "sending me to work" in a sense. Nevertheless, he took on the stay-at-home-dad role with ease as he worked to build his company, Elite Prototype Athletics.

It was hard to get my career in broadcasting off the ground in Michigan, and the last thing I wanted to do was just sit around all day while Devale was at practice. The pageant girl in me was good at getting my face together and helping other girls around me, too, so working at MAC came naturally for me. I felt so intimidated when I approached the MAC counter at Macy's Kings Plaza. I knew I had to step my game up and I was ready to learn as much as I could about the business and the artistry as fast as possible. There was opportunity for upper mobility within the company, so it was game time. Fortunately, I was able to snag an opening at Kings Plaza for a part-time artist, and within six months I had worked my way into management and was promoted to key holder at MAC Macy's in Manhasset and shortly after assistant manager at Roosevelt Field mall in Garden City, New York. Rising up through the ranks at MAC gave us steady health insurance and provided us with some financial cushion so that Devale could focus on building his business and going out for auditions and commercial work as it became available.

Devale

When Kay told me that she was pregnant with Jackson, it was like an immediate change in my ideas of what I had to do to become a father. As committed as I was to being a father, that focus didn't necessarily make me a better husband. My whole focus at that point was based on building my career to make as much money as possible. With my mind centered on our finances, I can be honest and say that I was not as emotionally and spiritually available as I could have been to Khadeen, especially during her pregnancy and when she was working full-time at MAC.

I always knew that I didn't want my wife to have to work full-time. I wanted her to be able to spend time at home with Jackson and make her moves as she saw fit, whether it was being a stay-at-home mom or pursuing her passions. But I knew she was working hard so that we could have health insurance after I was cut from the NFL. I knew it was just a means to an end, so I had to figure out a way to get more hours as an actor and become eligible to join the Screen Actors Guild and transfer the burden of health insurance from Khadeen to me.

When I got into my grind during that period, I was working eighteen hours a day, seven days a week. I literally only got home to go to sleep and then I woke up early to go back to work. It seemed like the right thing to do because I was being a provider, but I wasn't necessarily being a protector. I wasn't protecting Khadeen's mental health. I wasn't a protector of her heart and her spirit. I was in grind and self-loathing mode. It was horrible. When you're sleep deprived and working nonstop, you tell yourself that you have a right to be resentful in your relationship and you give yourself permission to not behave properly when you get home.

There were times when I came home and I wasn't always the best person. I was often irritable and angry. I was upset at myself because I wasn't where I wanted to be. I was upset at the world because I had followed all the rules and guidelines they told me you're supposed to follow to find success and be happy, and I wasn't. I had no one to blame but myself, but what do you do when you're young and immature and you're just trying to check off the boxes? You try to find someone else to blame in order to avoid looking in the mirror. And, of course, I blamed the closest person to me, Khadeen. So when I found out we were having our son, my focus shifted to make more money. And I know that didn't help me to become a better husband or even prepare me to be a better father.

Khadeen

A year after we had Jackson, I was still working at MAC and Devale was his sole caretaker. I knew that Devale took a lot of pride in being a stay-at-home dad and holding it down for our family. But I was so heartbroken because I was missing so many of Jackson's first milestones. As a new mom, all I wanted to do was be at home with my son. My commute to Garden City was forty-five minutes without traffic and I would be gone for twelve hours in the middle of the day from working a retail shift from one to ten at night. I took on a job that I wasn't necessarily happy with, but I knew it was a means to an end. I was exhausted, but I was careful not to complain about it too much because I didn't want Devale to feel bad. I knew he was trying to build something new from scratch. He would always remind me that working at MAC was a temporary sacrifice.

I remember one particular Thanksgiving season when retail hours were crazy, I left Thanksgiving dinner early because I had to open up the store for Black Friday. I put my head on Devale's chest and burst into tears. He let me cry for as long as I could before my shift and he said, "I promise you this is going to be your last holiday season of having to leave us to work in that store. These commercials are picking up and I am going to find a way to make it happen for our family."

One thing I can always be confident about with Devale is that he is a man of his word. I looked at him through my tears and replied, "I know." Deep down, I knew he was going to find a way for us to be able to shift gears and for me to be the more present wife and mother that I wanted to be. We wanted to be the best versions of ourselves as parents and as partners, but we didn't know exactly how that was going to happen.

Devale

Khadeen and I didn't have a true honeymoon period. We transitioned straight into becoming first-time parents and hustling to get our careers off the ground. When my NFL career ended, for the first time in my life the idea of being great at something was just an abstract thought. When you don't know what you don't know, it's scary and frustrating. There were times when I wasn't sure what to do, but seeing Khadeen's confidence in me was more than enough of an impetus for me to keep working toward my goals. It didn't matter how much money we had or what I had to borrow to pull us through. Khadeen always smiled when she saw me, and she held me down. I used to say to her, "Babe, you know I'm going to get us back to where we were when I was playing professional ball." Her reply was always the same: "I know." She wasn't condescending or dismissive. I believed that she believed in me, and that made me keep going.

Pivoting your entire life can be extremely scary, especially if you're doing it alone. If you stumble, there's no one there to catch you. But when you have a partner and they can maintain a certain part of the household while you pivot, you feel a little bit more comfortable taking chances.

Khadeen

I had to encourage Devale during this time because he was starting to feel the burden of not providing for us in the way that he wanted to. I wanted to create a safe space for him to know that it was okay and that I was going to be here for our family regardless of our circumstances. I knew that it was just a matter of time for us to get back on our feet after all the blows that we had endured. I wanted to continue having conversations with him and get on the same page about the plans we made for ourselves in college. As Devale was building his acting career, he was also developing his business, Elite Prototype Athletics. The company was designed to train young athletes. Devale always had a great business acumen and knew how to crunch out numbers quickly.

As I continued to work at MAC, Devale's confidence was building as he started taking more auditions and booking regional commercials. Slowly but surely, our money stressors began to alleviate and we didn't have to count every single penny. There were times when Devale would get a day rate of fifteen hundred dollars for a commercial and then a few weeks later he would get two or three residuals checks for a few thousand dollars. We had no idea that this money was coming our way.

I remember Devale looking at the breakdown from the Screen Actors Guild for how much he would need to make to qualify for health insurance. The number was just a little under four thousand dollars. Devale said, "When I make this money, you can quit MAC." Literally the next day, we were going into our building with an armful of groceries in one hand, laundry in the other, and somehow getting Jackson in the door with his stroller. Devale checked the mail before we headed upstairs, and sure enough, there was a check inside for the exact amount that he needed. I remember Devale saying, "I told you I was going to do it," and without missing a beat I said, "I know."

Once this milestone happened with Devale's acting career, I began working at MAC as a freelance makeup artist. Working freelance gave me the freedom to have more autonomy over my time and to build out my own business. I began providing makeup services to brides and wedding parties. I started linking up with wedding planners, and before I knew it, I was booked almost every weekend from April to October. I loved bridal makeup because I would receive a percentage of the fee for the trial makeup session and then the guaranteed balance on the wedding day. Combining my freelance work at MAC with the bridal makeup made me feel more confident that I was able to do more for Devale and Jackson. I was also feeling more confident as a businesswoman. When my business was booming with large wedding parties, I would bring my sister in as my assistant. It was fun to tag-team with someone I could trust.

I also started getting back in front of the camera with a news outlet called the Hot Zone USA. There were also some acting gigs that popped up and commercial auditions with Devale that we did as a couple and even a few that we did as a family with Jackson.

We were both feeling better about being in a space where we were doing the work that we wanted to do. When you're walking in your purpose and you're doing the things that you really love, it helps you to feel more hopeful and gives you confidence to keep moving toward a shared future together. Devale and I were no longer collapsing into exhaustion every day and coming home and unloading misery on each other. We felt like we were empowering each other and ourselves.

Now that we are twenty years into our relationship, our disagreements are shorter because we know how to communicate to get to the root of any issue quickly. One of the great things about having more experience with Devale under my belt is that we now understand that we are in this relationship to be of service to each other. We certainly didn't have the words or the understanding that this is what we were working toward in our first few years of marriage. But now we know the value of releasing ourselves from our individual agendas and thinking through how we can make each other's day better. I wake up every day and consider how I can alleviate some of Devale's stress or help his schedule be a little lighter that day. It's now a joy for me to adjust my mindset in this way because I know he's doing the same thing for me.

As much as I love my children, no one takes precedence over Devale because I know his love and commitment to me has brought us this far in our relationship. I know that he continues to look for ways to not just be of service to me but to make my life smoother, easier, and grander. We are so invested in each other's hopes and dreams that we're going to continue to find ways to support and uplift each other.

In retrospect, we needed that time in the first five years of our marriage to struggle and move through our rough patches. After dealing with those challenges, we were able to prosper and work through our difficulties with more ease, understanding, and grace for each other.

Devale

I'll never forget Thanksgiving Day 2011. Jackson was seven months old and it was our first holiday as a family of three. Kay was now a manager at MAC and had to be at the store in Roosevelt Field for the Black Friday rollout. We were eating dinner at her parents' house, but Kay had to leave because the mall was opening at eight p.m. She finished her plate and said goodbye to her family. I walked her to the door with Jax in my arms. Kay opened the door and then turned toward me. She pressed her forehead into my chest and said, "Booby, I hate this . . ." with tears rolling down her face. I lifted her chin with my left hand and said, "I promise this will be your last year working retail during the holidays." I kissed her lips and could taste the tears that pooled at the top of her mouth. She smiled at me and replied, "You promise?"

"Hell, yeah!" I replied. She looked me right in the eyes and said, "I know."

Kay kissed Jax on the cheek and turned to go to work. I watched her from behind the glass door until she took off and turned the corner. Tears were rolling down my face. I knew I had to go harder.

By November of our second year of marriage, I had booked a Kentucky Fried Chicken commercial that set me up to join the Screen Actors Guild and qualify us for health insurance. Right before Christmas, I told Khadeen that she could quit her job as a manager at MAC. I remember having this conversation with her in our car on St. Mark's Avenue in Brooklyn. I saw the fear in her eyes when she said, "Babe, I want to quit, but I'm not sure if I can."

I replied, "Khadeen, when I was growing my business, you had everything on lock. You gave me the ability to go out there and chase my dreams and build my business. You might not make as much in the beginning, but with the contacts you have at MAC, I know you'll make five times more when you focus on yourself and what you want to do."

All she could say then was "Baby, if you say I can do it, I will do it."

A few days before her birthday in early December, she resigned from working at MAC full-time, and she started building her own bridal makeup business. Within less than three months, Khadeen was making more money. By this point, I was now in the Screen Actors Guild and I had the insurance we needed to cover our family. But Khadeen would've never been able to take that leap of faith if she didn't know or trust that I had it.

If you choose not to be married, this doesn't mean you're a failure. It means that you have to look internally and say, "Do I want to be of service to someone else for the rest of my life?"

When you have two people working toward a common goal, when one person wants to make a leap of faith and they know and trust their partner to be the foundation, they can take that leap confidently. That leap of faith can allow them to grow exponentially—and lifts you up as well.

DEVALE AND KHADEEN'S HOT TAKE
Simpin' and Submitting

We're on social media, so we *know* folks got something to say about our definition of service in our marriage. Dudes like Devale are often called simps—or men who do whatever their women want—and women like Khadeen are often called submissive. *Simpin'* and *submitting* both have negative connotations—and it leaves no room for actual service in your relationship.

We know that a lot of people in this generation take pride in being a boss or a bad bitch—and there's nothing wrong with that. But we've learned through our relationship that when we've individually taken the time to know ourselves better, it's easier to lay down these societal labels and roles and focus on what's best for our relationship. It doesn't make Devale any less of a man to get our boys ready in the morning and take them to school. When Khadeen stepped up to be the primary breadwinner in our family during our first few years of marriage, that didn't threaten the dynamics of our relationship.

Don't let those social media "relationship experts" out there make you feel crazy or think you are weak for serving your partner. When you know who you are and what you are committed to in your relationship, service is a natural extension of your love for each other. And trust us—most of these folks pointing fingers and calling other people simps and submissives most likely aren't happy to begin with. So if you've got a person at home that you are happy simpin' and submitting with, stick with what works for you and let that service to each other become a strong foundation for your relationship.

Doing It and Doing It Well

When you are married for more than ten years, you might start to worry that you will begin to lose your physical attraction to your partner. What happens when one person feels like they are sacrificing their needs and desires for the other person? How do you even make time for sex after a full day of taking care of the kids, working a full-time job, or building a business, and just trying to take care of your own damn self in the process? And when you do finally make it to the bedroom, how do you stop your head from spinning around questions such as "Is he or she still attracted to me?" "Did I last long enough?" "Am I doing it right?" or "Is there something wrong with me?"

After four kids and building a few businesses, we know all too well how easily sex can get stale and feel like a chore. And sometimes it's not even for lack of desire or attraction; you are just exhausted from all the things in your day-to-day life. We can relate to the need to get away for just one night to reconnect. So before you give up hope in the bedroom, let's explore what it looks like to have real conversations about what you need, how to get real about your body and your life right now, and how to prioritize doing it and doing it well.

You Gotta Talk About It

Devale

When you get stuck in a cycle of not having sex the way you used to or when things start to slow down, it really starts to mess with your mind. Even if you do make it to the bed, your mind starts racing with questions like "Why is she slowing me down?" or "Does she even want to have sex with me right now?" I'm man enough to tell you that when Kay would dismiss me after our sons were born or I could tell she just wasn't in the mood, it was a blow to my ego. I would try to troubleshoot what was going on and force myself to get into the moment. But I found that when sex feels like a chore for us, that's the quickest way for one or both of us to shut down.

Khadeen made it very clear to me when we first started dating that she never wanted to be an option in my life, and she didn't want to share me with anyone—especially physically. I made it clear when we first started dating that I wasn't ready to be a boyfriend because I was young and wanted to explore my options living outside my parents' home for the first time. She shared the same sentiment but we couldn't stay away from each other, both physically and emotionally. I was drawn to her in a way that I wasn't to other women. So in my mind, I said, "Devale, why don't you just put all your energy into Kay?" She said she didn't want to be an option and that she didn't want to share me, so I figured she would be happy to know that I was only giving my body to her. So that's what I did, but she wasn't as happy as I thought she would be. And this is where the confusion came in.

I constantly had these thoughts running through my head: If you only want me to share my body with you, and you want me to constantly make you feel desired, why do you act as if it's a problem when I come to you for sex? It really doesn't make any sense. Here I am, giving you everything you asked for and you make it seem like I'm bothering you. But if I choose to go somewhere else, then I'm disregarding your feelings *and your body*. What about my feelings? What about my body?

We were both young and this was before we had kids, so I was truly perplexed. It seemed to me as if Kay wasn't thinking about me at all. She just wanted to have sex on her terms—when she wanted it, how she wanted it and, most importantly, only as often as she deemed was necessary. I'm gonna be totally honest and say that that's just not fair. It seemed to me that sex was only important to her when she wanted it to be a priority.

For example, if I was in the mood and she wasn't, then she would say things like, "Sex shouldn't always be a priority and not the most important aspect in a relationship." I got that and I would agree, but if I mentioned having sex with someone else since it's not really a priority, then she would say, "Sex is too important to share with an outside party." What the hell?! That seemed mad, selfish, and controlling. I was the one in our relationship with the higher sex drive, and so we constantly found ourselves in a cycle of being together versus not being together.

This problem didn't go away on its own and it remained a problem for our entire relationship as boyfriend and girlfriend, then our engagement, and even the early parts of our marriage. It is the biggest reason why we took so many breaks during our relationship. We wanted to see if there was someone out there more sexually compatible for each of us. But that never worked. We always found ourselves back together because our sexual chemistry is *amazing*! The naive boy in me felt that if I kept jumping through all the hoops she required as a woman, she would ultimately see that I'm investing in her long-term happiness and she would open up sexually. *Wrong!* All that did was make her feel like I would do everything she asked in every aspect of her life while simultaneously suppressing all the things I required as a partner. This was a *huge* mistake on my part because I lived like that in our relationship for over a decade.

What saved things for us and brought our sex life back was being able to talk about it. It took both of us being completely honest without fear of being judged or losing each other if we didn't agree on every single item. Through that Khadeen and I were able to figure out that her sex drive was being affected by the kind of birth control that she was taking. After our abortion in college, we made it a point to protect ourselves from pregnancy seeing as how we both hated condoms. She also discovered that she was having challenges hormonally with postpartum depression after each birth. There's no way in the world I would know that as a man unless we took the time to have that conversation.

It was also good for us to take the guilt and shame out of thinking that one person was at fault for something. Since college my sex drive has been consistently higher than Kay's. If I'm the one who's ready to get it in, I can't look at her and make her wrong for not feeling the same way. It's my work to get my ego out the way and find out what turns my wife on, both inside and outside the bedroom. I had to ask myself, "What am I doing that's good here?" or "What could I do better?" If she ain't feeling what I'm putting down, then I need to ask, "Why does she keep putting up a gate right now?" Asking yourself and your partner those questions never gets old. I do it all the time because I know how I am.

It doesn't take much for me to get in the mood. Kay walks by in shorts—I'm in the mood. Kay looks me in the eye for more than a second and a half—I'm in the mood. Kay brushes her teeth—I'm in the mood. One thing I always say is that I'm unapologetic about how much my wife turns me on and I *need* physical touch.

Listen and listen closely, even if things feel real stale for you, don't stop talking about what you need and what you desire. Let your wife know that you still think she's sexy. Let her know that you still want her. But also let her know what you need. She is just as much accountable for your happiness as you are for hers. The phrase "happy wife, happy life" is bullshit. You both are deserving of everything you want and require out of life. As long as you express it in a loving manner, you shouldn't feel ashamed by your truth. It doesn't matter how monotonous it seems, there's always breakthroughs when you have conversations. As monotonous as you think the conversation is, when you stop having a conversation, that's when it's over. When you stop talking about sex, that's when you should be worried.

Khadeen

"When's the last time you touched me?" That is usually the way the conversation would start and it was a surefire way to turn me all the way off. So you want to have sex, but now you've made it crazy awkward, and we definitely won't be doing anything but discussing the latest sex timeline. Knowing that I could not back down from the conversation, I would start to do the calculations in my head. "Today is Thursday, yesterday I closed the counter at work so I know we went right to sleep. Tuesday, I think we left our parents' house late so—" Then he would cut me off and blurt out "*Sunday, Kay!* We had sex on Sunday and now it's Thursday! What am I supposed to do with that?" Some days I would reply to myself, "Damn! How do you remember that? Because I barely remember what I had for breakfast." One thing about Devale—he's going to exercise his middle school debate team strategies and want to debate and discuss for hours. For me, that would just make for more draining conversations that would end in no resolve, lonely nights while in the same bed, and for damn sure, no sex.

At first, when we would have these discussions, the minute I heard the word *sex*, I would just mentally check out and shut down. At this point, the "air" around sex was forced and negative. I would roll my eyes and think, "Here we go again." But the more we talked, the more I began to understand that Devale wasn't pressuring me for his own needs per se—he genuinely wanted to connect with me and wanted to make sure that he was doing his part to ensure that I was still into him. He so desperately wanted Khadeen, his college girlfriend, back but to be honest she was nowhere to be found. This was never for lack of attraction to him. Instead, I was drained and much of my focus was on trying to be a stellar mom and hustling to make sure we would be able to one day get ourselves out of our Brooklyn apartment. After having our middle boys only fifteen months apart, I was feeling touched out. I either had a baby in me, one on my breast, or both, and the last thing I was in the mood for was anything or anyone penetrating me. Plus, I was still coming to terms with my new body post-baby and though I knew that he still found me desirable, I was still far from being in the mood. At times, I would feel super inadequate and wondered if something was wrong with me internally. I mean, it *had* to be something.

I remember calling a friend of mine who is a bit older than me and confiding in her about this sexual anxiety that I developed. The truth is I so desperately yearned to be what my husband needed and at this point, I was willing to try anything. She sent me an address to see a man named Blacka at a health food store in the Bronx. Now one thing about Brooklyn heads—we don't electively travel to the Bronx but again, desperation. So I did the unthinkable that weekend and hauled ass to link up with Blacka. I was giddy as I pulled up. I was like a kid on her way to the bodega with some change for hot cheese popcorn, some Chick-O-Sticks, and an Arizona iced tea. Blacka's spot was a small, unassuming storefront under a train track, and I was greeted by the scents of frankincense, myrrh, and other essences mixed with a little ganja. "Ahh a yardie's spot," I thought to myself as an older yet statuesque Jamaican gentleman with salt-and-pepper locks and a beard emerged from behind the counter. Upon seeing him and his physique I thought to myself, "He looks like he knows what he's talking about!" Either that or he found the fountain of youth. I told Blacka who sent me and he warmly welcomed me on some family vibes. It wasn't the easiest thing to divulge to him my libido troubles but he proceeded to show me the goods that I needed. It's like he knew why I was there. I thought to myself, "Damn, is it really written all over my face that I haven't been putting it down in the bedroom?!" Nevertheless, I didn't take offense, and later found out that that was his specialty—all-natural, herbal, and root concoctions that have been proven to save marriages one bottle at a time. Apparently, folks had been traveling from near and far for the goodies that only Blacka could supply. He even had some supplement suggestions, such as maca root that he claimed would aid me in getting that old thang back. Truth be told, I gave the goods a try and it showed some changes but not enough to convince me. Turns out it worked more with men than women and Lord knows Devale didn't need any more of a boost. I wanted to get to the root of my problem in order to remedy it versus using Band-Aids. On a follow-up conversation with the same friend who introduced me to Blacka, she said, "Be kind to yourself, Khadeen. You aren't out of the postpartum woods just yet. It takes the body a full year to get back to normal." I welcomed her kind words of comfort and prayed for some internal change because this was not it. Fast-forward to present day. I had to recognize that nearly two decades into our relation-ship, we don't have that newness factor of discovering each other's bodies like the way we did when we were in college. So we really had to work on keeping the lines of communica-tion open and get curious—and stay curious—about what we like about each other physically now. Things have a way of changing over time and I learned to appreciate Devale's conversations about sex as him being honest and actively working on our sex life. I learned that not everything was an attack and over time, we developed a way of talking to each other where the approach was more entrenched in love and not frustration. This was a major improvement for us.

I realized, too, that new environments, travel, and discov-ering new things together was sexy to me. Then add bae to the mix and it's a recipe for some good ol' bones jumping. Nothing turns me on more than uncovering something new about my husband and then discovering how I can enjoy that with him. I've noticed that when we take on a new adventure together, Devale and I come alive again. We've deduced that unplugged time away from the stresses of life is our strongest catalyst for reconnection. Because let's be real, I love my man and want nothing more than for him to be content and ful-filled in this life that we share together. Much of my lack of attention on him was mainly due to my attention being di-vided up and spread thin with kids, work, and family. I also expected him to just understand because he's an adult and that's what adults do. But that can wear thin with anyone. So when Devale asked me, "Damn, so I have to spend money and take you away to get my girlfriend back?" I smiled and retorted, "Hell, yeah! Every now and again. Sounds like a fair exchange to me! Where to next?!"

I remember when Devale and I took a trip to the Jade Mountain in St. Lucia and we ran to the top of the summit instead of taking a bus. Just taking on that different level of physical activity got our pheromones going and that night it definitely invigorated our time in the bedroom. And to be fair, it was hard not to want to do anything but be naked and make love all day long out there. This place oozed love, seclusion, and romance. Our room was completely outdoor and tucked away, facing the beautiful, scenic landmark Pitons. I'm not telling you to climb to the top of a mountain. But I would recommend taking a day to work out with each other in the gym or trying out a new fun activity together. Giving ourselves the space to talk about who we are now and to spark our bodies in different ways definitely has helped us to get to the other side of those still moments in our sex life.

KHADEEN'S HOT TAKE
Don't Be Afraid to Get to the Root

If you know that things aren't feeling the way they used to in the bedroom, you have to be relentless about getting to the root of your problem. When you're focusing on getting that spark back, you have to be willing to go the extra mile, put your ego aside, and take a good, hard, honest look at your health and well-being.

When I was going through my challenges with switching up my birth control and then moving through postpartum depression after each birth with my sons, it was heartbreaking for me that I just wasn't feeling inspired or motivated to have sex. I knew that my husband deserved more, but he just wasn't getting the best of me. During those phases in our sex life, I just felt like I didn't have anything else to give. I'm super grateful that Devale was patient with me and that he hung in there until I felt like myself again.

If this is the person who you are committed to creating your life with, you can't be ashamed to have the honest conversations, go to therapy if needed, take on those extra doctors' appointments, and get to the bottom of what's missing. It might be as simple as changing up something in your diet or taking just one night away to get out of your everyday routine. Whatever it is, be committed to getting to the root of your problem so that you can get back to that good lovin'.

Respect the Stages of Intimacy

Devale

When you're with someone for a long time, you gotta realize that there are different stages to your intimacy. Khadeen and I were good with the physical act of full-on, animalistic sex in our college days and up until our first few years of marriage. I used to throw Kay all over the room, put her in different positions, and mix things up with hard-core, rough, and extremely long lovemaking sessions. We would both lie there sweaty, exhausted, and proud that we could play out all our wildest sexual fantasies with each other in a safe way. That is why we both value monogamy so much—because we are both nasty freaks. But sex is a whole different ball game when you're thinking about mortgages, tuition, new babies, aging parents, or building businesses. It was much harder for Khadeen and me to feel sexy when I was released from the NFL or when she was working around the clock as a makeup artist at MAC. We have a little minute before we get all these boys out of the house, but we've got a feeling our sex life is going to change again once we become empty nesters. With every season of your life, you gotta be patient with your partner and realize that these changes are going to affect your sex life, too.

One thing that is a *scientific fact* is that a woman's reproductive health directly affects her sex drive. As men, we don't deal with anywhere near as many changes to our bodies from adolescence to menopause. So as I matured as a man I learned to understand the female body and assist in what is required to put my wife in a place to be sexual when I want sex. It sounds like a lot of work, but I don't have periods every month and I didn't have to carry four children so this is what I equate to me doing my part. This way we both win.

Turning your spouse on also includes constantly being in service—and not just to get something in return. When you are constantly in service to your spouse, they are going to naturally want to reciprocate. Once your partner is willing to naturally reciprocate, that action is going to work its way to the bedroom without fail.

Khadeen

I can tell you that during month nine of each of my pregnancies, that's when I felt my worst—but ironically, that's when Devale found me to be the sexiest. I didn't see anything sexy about having huge breasts and a swollen vagina. All I was thinking about was "I got a baby inside of me," and the last thing I wanted was somebody touching me. Not sure if this is a thing but I was beginning to feel touched out. I was tired of having someone touching me, tired of having someone in me, tired of having someone at my breast—much less a husband who is looking to do all of the above! I should be thrilled at the fact that my husband sees me as this beautiful sexual goddess no matter the phase I'm in.

Whether I'm not pregnant, about-to-pop pregnant, or fresh out of delivery, Devale is ready to go. Me—not so much. By my fourth pregnancy with Dakota, I had to realize that his sexual needs did not necessarily need to be indicative of my desire. As my pregnancy progressed, I was in a beautiful space in life. We had moved into our new home in Georgia, I was comfortable with where we were financially, my mom and dad pretty much lived with us full time, and Devale made every provision to ensure that I could relax and enjoy this last pregnancy. Because I was in such bliss, I was then naturally feeling the urge to make sure that he was taken care of as well.

That's the beauty and reciprocity in service. The feeling of being heard, seen, and understood is a turn on. When I no longer wanted to be penetrated, I resorted to other means to make sure he was sexually satisfied. And baby, I have two words for you—lock jaw! No complaints from Mr. Ellis and I had it down to a science. But with each pregnancy, I learned to be patient with myself as I got to this final phase. I would be exhausted and my mind was already thinking ahead to labor, delivery, and bringing my baby home safely. With every phase of our intimacy, Devale and I have learned what things are a green light, yellow light, or red light in the bedroom for us. Something that was a green light before we had kids might be a red light now. After having multiple kids, there are definitely some things that are a red light for me now—and will never be a green light again. But that's okay because it's fun discovering new green lights.

I finally got to a point where I didn't want to blame anyone or anything else for not feeling sexy. I went through every stage of blaming Devale, blaming the kids, and blaming myself about what wasn't working for me. I didn't want Devale to feel like he was unwanted or neglected, or that I was no longer able to meet his needs in that department. I knew that our sex life was something that mattered to me and I was willing to do the work and the research to get to the root of what was challenging for me and get back to feeling like myself again. It took a minute, but it feels good to take it back to a place where we feel whole and connected again.

Your sex life will definitely evolve, especially if you've been together and married for a while. It takes practice and understanding to continue having conversations and keep an open mind to try new things.

Take It Somewhere New

Khadeen

Ships passing in the night. That's the only way I can describe the monotony that was our sex life. And to be honest, life in general. Being bogged down by the every day hustle and bustle of life can be daunting, not just as an individual, but when you're trying to do life with your partner, it manifests itself differently for each party.

For me, when things get hectic, I try to spread out and cover as many bases as possible to get things done, knowing that it may require me to focus on everything but my husband in the moment.

Devale functions completely differently. In those moments, he still needs to be seen. I used to look at him sideways and think, "You're an adult. You should understand that we have all these things happening right now and we just may have to wait." Devale's reply is usually something like, "Well, if you were more efficient with getting things done in a timely manner then you would have more time for the things you want." Noted.

He had a point. And how long was I supposed to expect my husband to just sit back and understand all the time? When was I going to say no, my husband comes first or, let me get this done now rather than putting it off because it will free up time for later. I had to check myself. My husband should not have to beg for my time or vie for attention. And to be clear, I should worry if he was not checking for me. That disconnect was never an option and I had to fix it.

When you've been married for a while, it can be very easy to get stuck in your daily routine of taking care of home and raising your kids, and before you know it, you're in a sexual rut with your partner. One of the ways that Devale and I started mixing things up is that we started taking little weekend getaways. Even when we were living in Brooklyn, we would give ourselves the treat of crossing the bridge to spend a night in Manhattan. It was a lot of fun to be in a hotel room or to do something outside of our day-to-day schedule. For me, having the ability to escape and create that kind of environment made me feel more adventurous.

There was one weekend we spent in Manhattan where we completely let loose and I noticed that I felt like I released a lot of negativity and tension from my body. After taking that time to intentionally connect with Devale, I thought, "*Wow!* It feels like we are in a much better place." It was refreshing to reconnect with him, be present, and enjoy our sex life.

For a while, having sex in my marriage came with this negative cloud around it. I would think, "Oh, damn, it's rolling on to day two since we've had sex, so I know I'm going to have to do it again soon." I knew I had gotten too comfortable with thinking that way when it put a bad taste in my mouth to think about sex like a chore.

Planning a short getaway, even just for twenty-four hours, made me look forward to getting into a headspace and a physical space where I could get down and have sex the way that I wanted to. I don't know about you, but I love that animalistic attraction where you are not planning to go at it, but when you do, it feels like the thrill of having sex in your parents' room and enjoying that moment before they come home.

When you get out of that normal routine, having sex in a new environment makes you feel like a kid again. There are certain cares that you can put away whenever you are on vacation. After a few days of raw, animalistic sex, it inspires you to drop it like it's hot when you come back home. Without fail, Devale and I are always in a better space when we escape for a little while. We're more aligned with our service to each other and we have more space to think about the future.

Now that we are more intentional about having that time away, I feel like our sex life at home is more organic. It's way more authentic because we're really tuned in to each other. We spend days where we're just walking past each other and we also have these beautiful flirtatious moments where we let each other know without saying a word, "I see you." Those moments of intimacy that I have with Devale throughout the day, although they are quick, culminate in a more fulfilling sex life, which I am enjoying more every day.

Devale

I've learned with Khadeen that she has to escape from our kids in order to truly be present with me sexually. Even when we're away on vacation, if the kids are in the room or somewhere nearby where she can hear them, she's always going to be thinking about them. The only time I can really get her to focus on just being in the moment is if our kids are nowhere in her vicinity.

I remember that I used to have this constant argument with Khadeen where I would say, "Why do I have to spend thousands of dollars on a vacation to get my wife back?" It felt unfair that the only way I could get her attention was to spend money and plan a trip. But I discovered that by having these intentional one- or two-night escapes, it helped us to bond more and connect by creating these new experiences together.

DEVALE'S HOT TAKE
Kick the Kids Out of the Bed

I'm not ashamed to say it—I regularly kick my kids out of the bed, y'all. I know Khadeen likes to cuddle with them and make sure that they get that good quality mommy time. But me—I give them that good cuddle time and then they gotta go!

Our oldest son, Jackson, was in the bed with us for a long time. Like most first-time parents, it was more convenient for us to have him in the same bed with us for nursing and late-night diaper changes. Because we weren't deliberate with putting a time limit on how long he was in the bed with us, in all honesty he probably slept with us a little longer than he should have. By the time we had our second son, Kairo, we knew from our experience with Jackson that we didn't want to get in the habit of letting him sleep with us. We put him in the bassinet right away. We did the same thing with Kaz and Dakota, too.

Khadeen and I have discovered that it's more empowering for our boys to figure out how to self-soothe themselves during the night. Now we ain't going to let them cry their heads off, but we've learned to cut off some of those extra trips to the bathroom and the request for one more story by giving them the space to figure out how to comfort themselves.

Most of the time when I'm talking with parents who have issues with moving their child into their own beds, it's the parents who don't want the separation and not necessarily the kids. One or both parents feel more comfortable with knowing that the kid is nearby. But real talk here: You can't start these kinds of habits with your kids, especially if you want to maintain a regular sex life.

You Have to Prioritize Your Pleasure

Khadeen

Shit it's Wednesday! I could already tell by Devale's mood that I am a day late with giving it up. It's pretty amazing how a man's entire mood can be fucked up if he's backed up. And I mean backed up by two to three days. Meanwhile, I'm still on a high from the last session. So I backtrack in my mind last time we had sex—Sunday. Damn. That's one day too many in between. It used to make me wonder if I wasn't putting it down properly.

I mean listen, one time in particular, I pulled out all the stops. We were returning to our home in Calabasas after staying at my parents' and his parents' home in Brooklyn for a week. As a family of five at the time, we easily outgrew our parents' homes and no longer had our apartment in Crown Heights. So quiet sex sessions in my old room and quickies were the only way to get by while we were bumming a stay off at the parents. We also noted that in the future, we just had to get a hotel room whenever we were visiting home because it was all too overwhelming.

I asked Devale what he wanted me to do for him sexually when we got back home. I was ready to bust it wide open and make up for a long week. He requested a school girl outfit, heels, and a pair of color contacts that I had worn over our stay in New York for a photo shoot. Not knowing anything about how to store contacts, I put them in the container with water instead of contact solution. Mistake number one. Then I was unable to get them back into my eyes. I got a cute off-white lace bodysuit that looked the bomb on me from Savage X Fenty, and this was going to be my moment to perform. My enthusiasm was met with limp dick and judgment when

I pranced out in my Fenty trying to play savage. Devale proceeded to tell me that I did not do as he requested, and, therefore, it killed the mood for him. "Where are the contacts? That's not a skirt." This escalated into an argument, and, of course, the mood was killed and sex was no longer on the table. He even had the nerve to go in my closet and dismantle all the shoes that I had so nicely placed on display. The kicker—he did all this with his dick on medium. The nerve. How are you pissed off and horny simultaneously?

We ended up laughing uncontrollably about the fact that he was big-mad at me, threw my shoes around, and had the gall to do it all on medium. This is really when I realized that men have little control over their hormones. After laughing about it, we eventually got the mood back and had an amazing session.

I say that to say I'm learning that I need to give him what he wants. If he asks for something specifically, there's no need to try to re-create the request coated in whatever I feel is best or convenient.

Devale

In my teenage years, I thought that the harder I was or the longer I could last, the more she's going to orgasm. Like most boys growing up, my sex education was the Spice channel and Pornhub. When I became an adult, started listening to women, and did my own research, I found out that most women do not orgasm from penetration alone. Most women need some form of clitoral stimulation during sex. So, fellas, you got to put your ego aside and realize that if you really want to please a woman, it can't be about you.

Khadeen is more private than I am about some things in our sex life because she likes for some things to remain for the imagination. But when she asks me to try something new, I'm game. Whatever she wants, she's my wife and it's my responsibility to give her the pleasure that she wants and deserves. And at this point in our relationship, she is the same way about me. *Trust!*

The Kids Ain't First

You might be surprised to hear us say this, but we do not put our kids first. They're cute and all, but the biggest lesson we learned in the first five years of our marriage, and especially with our oldest son, Jackson, is that when we put all the focus on him, we created a toxic environment where it was very hard for us to figure out how to balance being good partners and being good parents. It wasn't until Khadeen was pregnant with our second son, Kairo, that we understood that we had to shift the energy to who we were as a couple first so that we could be the best parents to our sons. Now that we have added Kaz and Dakota to the family, it's incredibly important for us to show them a healthy relationship that will then allow them to seek out their own healthy relationships in the future.

When we became parents, we quickly understood that

our service for each other had to widen and expand so that we could build a strong legacy for our sons that would outlast our goals and aspirations. We also realized that we wanted to create a peaceful and healthier environment for our sons that allowed them to freely express their emotions, respectfully disagree with us, and develop their own voices. We wanted to build our home as a haven for our extended family to enjoy celebrations, experience and learn through disappointments, and build during our growing moments with us. Discovering how to build a home with a strong legacy, loyalty, and peace was quite the journey for us. We had to learn how to be flexible as our careers grew and evolved. And as our family has increased and our boys have become young men, we've had to learn how to stay nimble and give them the freedom to be who they want to be. A lot of our legacy building came through the process of taking control of our birthing experiences and uncovering our strengths as parents.

We definitely don't have all the answers, but we have learned a thing or two about what it takes to be present with our sons, give them plenty of room to try and to fail, and always make sure that we are a safe refuge for them. Let's dig into what it looks like to be a millennial parent so that you can, we hope, take a little something away from our victories and our challenges.

Here We Go! Starting the Adventure of a Lifetime

Devale

I'll **never forget** the phone call from Khadeen telling me that Jackson was on the way. She told me that she was going to the hospital because the doctor believed that she had preeclampsia. Her enzymes were elevated, so she was recommending that Khadeen be induced. Khadeen confirmed that she was going to be admitted and I finished training my students for the day and headed over to the hospital.

When I arrived, an older nurse was prepping Khadeen for an epidural. As the nurse was preparing the needle, she asked me if I needed to take a seat. I told her that I had multiple tattoos, so I was good with seeing needles—or so I thought. When she pulled that needle out, both of my legs got weak. I didn't know what was happening. I felt like I was blacking out and I wanted to run to the bathroom. Before I could jet, Khadeen grabbed me and said, "You're not going anywhere. You're going to stay right here."

It took the nurse three tries to get the needle in properly. Then she gave Khadeen the medication to be induced, and we waited overnight to see if the baby would come on its own. Early the next morning when the doctor checked Khadeen, she told us that we still had plenty of time before the baby came and that we should get something to eat.

I persisted with her and said, "Khadeen's not feeling the greatest. She says she feels a lot of pressure down there. I know my baby. If she's saying she feels it down there, this baby may be coming sooner than later."

The doctor casually said, "I've done this a bunch of times. I'm going to go get a coffee and I'll be back."

As the doctor left, I was looking at Khadeen, worried. Khadeen said, "Devale, I feel pressure," and she started to push. I looked down and all of a sudden Jackson was crowning. I ran to get the nurse and Khadeen's doctor. As soon as the doctor came back, Khadeen pushed two times and Jackson was out.

We knew from the sonogram that Jackson was going to be born with a clubfoot. As soon as he came out, the doctor and all the nurses grabbed him to prepare a boot for his foot. When I looked back at Khadeen, she looked a little gray and she was going in and out of consciousness. She reassured me that she was just tired. I checked between her legs to make sure everything was good. When I looked down there, it looked like *The Texas Chainsaw Massacre*. There was blood everywhere.

I called her mom, who is a nurse, back into the room and I said, "Does this look normal?" Her mother emphatically said, "No, that doesn't look normal." We called the nurse and the doctor and they came back in. Everyone then started screaming, "Prepare the operating room!" They wheeled Khadeen into an operating room, and I was frantically asking, "What's going on?" No one was saying anything to me. I vaguely remember sitting down with my mom because apparently I blacked out. My mom had to calm me down as tears started to roll down my face. I remember being pissed and thinking, "Is this one of those moments where I'm going to have my child, but I won't have my wife anymore?"

When they rolled Khadeen away, I thought about every bad movie scene I'd seen where everything goes horribly wrong. As this medical emergency was unfolding, I was upset because no one was telling me what was going on. They whisked my son away because of his foot, then they just took my wife away, and no one was answering me. I know they had to move quickly, but still, no one stopped to give me any information.

A few hours later, I remember waking up from a nap and then hearing the doctor confirm that Khadeen was out of surgery and everything was fine. Fortunately, she didn't need a blood transfusion. She had an internal tear in her cervix, and she needed twenty-four stitches in order to stop the bleeding. She was hemorrhaging, but they stopped the bleeding, and by the grace of God Khadeen was all right. I remember in that moment feeling like "If we get out of this unscathed, and Khadeen and the baby are fine, I don't want to have any more kids."

Khadeen

During week 37 of my first pregnancy, my doctor took some blood work and saw that my liver enzymes were elevated. She wasn't quite sure at the time what was causing it. It could have been early preeclampsia, but she wasn't 100 percent confident. She recommended inducing the baby because he was large enough to deliver safely at that point.

Once I got to the hospital, I felt like I was coerced into having an epidural. The nurse convinced me that my labor could be long and painful. She told me, "Maybe you should think about getting an epidural. Once the pain starts to kick in, you probably won't be able to withstand it."

It was my first child, so I was hanging on to every word that the medical professionals were telling me. You hear about labor pain. You don't know how bad it's going to be until you're in it—and I was about to be in it. So I went ahead and had the epidural. But I promise you if I catch this woman on the street to this day, I'm fighting her because I had such a bad experience with it.

The nurse who administered my epidural stuck me three different times. Each time she stuck me, I felt as if I was being electrocuted on the right side of my body. Whatever nerve she was hitting in my spine was causing this involuntary jolting of my body on one side. I was just so terrified that I was going to be paralyzed. I remember Devale seeing the needle and saying he needed to run to the bathroom. I said, "To the bathroom? You're not going to leave my side!" I remember putting his head on my shoulder and holding on to him for dear life. After three injections, she finally got the epidural in. But it was never in properly because I still felt a lot of the discomfort that I wasn't supposed to be feeling. I finally dilated to 10 centimeters and I began to push. The doctor didn't think that the baby was going to come as soon as he did, but sure enough, Jackson was en route.

After delivery, I felt exhausted and I was going in and out of consciousness. I initially thought that's that was what you're supposed to feel when you have a baby. I had just pushed a human out of a hole the size of an apricot that eventually became the size of a watermelon. Anybody would be tired and delirious after that. However, I was bleeding a lot. Devale and my mom confirmed that the amount of blood that they saw did not look normal. My doctor came back in and she discovered that my cervix had torn internally. I was immediately taken into emergency surgery.

During the emergency surgery, once I was in the OR, my legs were in the stirrups that held them open and up in the air. I remember an anesthesiologist being right behind me and trying to get my mind off things. Right before I became unconscious, I remember a team of medical students coming into the room because apparently my surgery was very rare. All I could think about was my bloody vagina with my legs open to a bunch of strange doctors. But when you're in the middle of fighting for your life, being embarrassed or ashamed is the last thing you should be thinking of.

As I was going into surgery, I was really focused on Jackson. We knew at five months that his left foot was clubbed. I remember thinking, "Oh my God, how long am I going to be in surgery? How long am I going to be away from my baby?" I told Devale to go with the baby and make sure he was okay. I didn't realize in that moment how severe my case was. All I could think about in that moment was that I needed to just make it back out.

When I woke up in the recovery room, I remember a very sweet nurse coming to me and saying, "You're out of surgery. Everything is fine. We're going to watch you for a little bit to make sure that you come out of the anesthesia properly. You're okay to go up to the mother and baby unit." Once the nurse reassured me that everything was okay, I was anxious to get to the baby and Devale. I was more worried about Devale and how he felt.

So many things come into perspective when you have a near-death experience. After my birthing experience, I learned that I was one step away from needing a blood transfusion. That's how much blood I lost from the tearing with Jackson. I was in the hospital for about eight days because I had to get my blood count back up. I remember Devale and I weeping together in my hospital room. You hear all the time about how a mother can be lost during labor, but you never ever think it's going to be you.

Take Charge of Your Birth Story

Khadeen

We were at Devale's parents' house when I went into labor with our second son, Kairo, because our apartment was undergoing renovations. I wasn't necessarily ready for him, but my water broke at 6:45 a.m. It was about thirty-seven weeks and two days. I went on with my day like normal. I woke up and got Jackson ready for school. I drove from Canarsie, where our family lives, into Crown Heights to drop Jackson off at school. I remember going back to my in-laws' house, taking a shower, and then I lost my mucus plug. My water was continuing to break, but I was still managing my contractions. We gathered everything we needed from the apartment, and I remember feeling the baby drop down into my pelvis. I said to Devale, "I think we should go to the hospital—NOW."

We got into the car and were promptly stuck in midday, after-school traffic in Brooklyn. The hospital was fifteen minutes away, but it took us almost an hour to get there. When Devale finally pulled up to the ER entrance, my sister ran to get me a wheelchair. I said, "Devale, don't look for parking.

Just come upstairs because I feel like something is happening. I'm scared and I don't want you to miss anything." My contractions were now coming back to back.

When my sister returned with the wheelchair, I was trying to keep my composure because I was in the hallway with random people. When I finally got to the triage unit, I was put in a room because my labor was starting. The doctor told me to open my legs, but I ignored him because Devale was not upstairs yet. I heard the doctor saying to my sister, "Is she hard of hearing? Does she need a translator? Do I need sign language?" I screamed back, "No, I'm ignoring you because my husband is not here. I don't want him to miss this because I feel like if I open my legs, something might happen."

The doctor and the nurse in the triage area were not taking my ignoring them lightly at this point. They both each grabbed one of my knees and Kairo flew out. Devale came down the hallway literally thirty seconds later. He entered the room and said, "Oh my God, are you kidding me? I just missed it." After that frantic feeling I had in the car and being wheeled off to triage, I could have avoided all of that if I'd been at home and just naturally had the baby in a calm environment. For our third son, Kaz, I opted for a home birth.

Devale

So many people are afraid to consult their ob-gyn about home births because they're afraid they're going to get a negative response. After missing Kairo being born because of the terrible parking situation in Brooklyn, Kay and I decided that it might be a better idea to have Kaz at home. Kairo was crowning in the car and the only reason why he didn't come out then was because Kay kept her legs crossed waiting for me to get to the hospital. On top of that, the hospital billed us upward of $25,000 for having the baby in triage and kicking us out a day later because we refused to accept any additional treatment. To be honest, we really didn't need them. Both her mom and my mom were very experienced with having three natural births each, so we felt very secure in the experience around us.

In deciding to have a home birth with Kaz, I made it a purpose to educate myself on *everything* related to prenatal, delivery, and postpartum care. Once again, I was choosing to be of service to my wife, who had the divine task of carrying and ushering another Ellis boy into the world. Kaz was our only surprise baby. We got pregnant with Kaz while Kay was still nursing Kairo. *Write this down.* If your doctor tells you it's very difficult to get pregnant while breastfeeding, they are lying. We never expected to raise three boys in that apartment, but I believe that God will never give you more than you can handle—and always everything you need. So in a lot of ways I see Kaz as one of our biggest blessings. His birth story brought Kay and I so close. We can write a whole other book on the home birthing process so I'll spare y'all the details, but Kaz entered the world as peaceful and safely as the baby Jesus in Bethlehem. Of course, without the hay and all that other shit. There was water, music, and family but no three wise men. Just our immediate families waiting in the living room watching *Dennis the Menace* with Jax and Ro waiting for their little brother to get here.

We had Kairo and then Kaz in New York, which is more liberal when it comes to home birthing. When we moved to Georgia to have our fourth son, Dakota, Khadeen's ob-gyn was not as liberal and not as welcoming to the home-birthing experience. She was very cold and dismissive, and it turned Khadeen off in a lot of ways to the health practices in Georgia.

The first thing that I would tell a woman looking to have a home birth is to speak to your doctor and find out if you're a good candidate for a home birth. We got a blessing from our doctor in New York, Dr. Veca, who assured us that Khadeen was a great candidate for home birthing.

Do as much research as you can on your own and watch as many home-birthing documentaries as you can stand. As long as you're prepared for the worst and the best scenarios, and you've sat down with your doula and midwife to create a birthing plan, you'll be fine.

After nearly losing Khadeen during the birth of our first son, I realized how emotionally, mentally, spiritually, and sometimes physically unavailable I was to my wife. I told Khadeen, "We've made a decision to have another child, and I want to be there 100 percent. Whatever you want and whatever you need, I will be there to support you."

From there, I chose to dedicate my energy to being of service to her in every aspect of her life. Anything she needed, if it was within my power, I was going to find a way to do it. If it wasn't within my power, I was going to find someone or some way to get it done.

I became a better husband and a better person. I realized how much that love was reciprocated when I started to become of service to her. When I started to focus on being what my partner needed, I realized that our marriage became fuller and happier. We were able to sustain that happiness because not only was I working on being a better version of myself for her, but she was also working on being a better version of herself for me. That doesn't mean we didn't stumble at times, but coming back to this concept is what saved us, time and time again.

Khadeen

Choosing to have a home birth with Kaz went against the wishes of a lot of our friends and family. As a nurse, my mom bought into the science of the traditional hospital route. I completely understood her reservations and her apprehension about the whole experience. But I just had such a good feeling and I had such trust in my midwife and her expertise. Everything that we spoke about in that meeting heavily led to me having this home birth.

Another tipping point for me in choosing a home birth

was the hospital restrictions. There were limitations on how many people I could have in the room and restrictions on taking photos and home videos. I wanted the opportunity to have as many people as I felt comfortable in the room with me, and I wanted to document my memories. We also had people being invested in our story with Kairo and then following my pregnancy with Kaz. I knew that my experience could show a different way of doing a home birth safely within the Black community.

I believe that my body was made and equipped to do what it naturally should do when it comes to having a baby. I'm not saying that there isn't a value in hospitals or in doctors. They are very necessary, especially in emergency situations. But based on my history with labors and deliveries, this was the right situation for me and my family. I don't have any regrets about hiring Takiya to be my midwife for my two youngest sons.

The biggest lesson that I took away from my entire experience dealing with a midwife is that it is so important for women to advocate for ourselves. If you're not equipped to do so, make sure that your partner, your spouse, or a doula is there to be that advocate for you. Naturally, there are things with labor that you're not able to control. But if you are in a position to be able to set out your wants and desires during birth, take that route, if you can.

With a home-birthing experience, everything is centered around the expectant mom, the expectant dad, and the family. Everyone feels like they have a place in the birthing experience. I also love that Takiya empowered me and gave me faith in my ability to have my babies. Any time I would say, "When you deliver the baby . . . ," she was quick to correct me and say, "I'm not delivering the baby. You're delivering your baby. I'm just here to support you." I can't tell you how powerful that was for me as a woman to hear.

KHADEEN'S HOT TAKE
Every Woman Deserves to Feel Safe and Protected

Every woman bringing life into this world deserves to feel that safe and protected. It took us till the last baby to get this right, but this last pregnancy, labor, and delivery experience was the best one. A big part of what made Dakota's arrival into the world so good for me was because Devale worked his ass off day in and day out to make sure that I was comfortable. He made sure that I didn't want or need for anything. He found a way to bend over backward to make everything happen—including being a stellar father for Jackson, Kairo, and Kaz, filming two seasons for two separate shows, and still making our house feel like a home.

I couldn't have predicted what a great father and provider he was going to be for our family back when we were dating at Hofstra. But more than what he provides as a husband and a father, it feels good to be with a man who makes me feel safe and protects me both physically and emotionally. I didn't think we were going to have another child after the traumatic birthing experience that I had with Jackson. But having Devale be so present and attentive to what I needed in terms of having a doula and a midwife and being willing to take an active role in my birthing experiences made me feel more comfortable with expanding our family.

Many people who claim to be "dating experts" on Instagram skip over the importance of a woman's need to feel safe and protected. This is not to say that a woman needs a man to show up as a knight in shining armor. But it does make all the difference in the world when you know that you have a partner who will physically, spiritually, and emotionally give you the support you need in whatever you're pursuing. I wouldn't have had the confidence to pursue my dreams of getting back into the beauty industry or putting myself out there on social media if I didn't have Devale as my husband. Every woman deserves to feel that kind of safety and protection.

Every Child Is Different

Khadeen

When you have your first child, you are overprepared for every scenario. Devale and I put every single thing we could think of on our baby registry, and we were incredibly fortunate that we were surrounded with so much love from our family and friends who got us everything we needed and more. Now that I've gone through this four times, it's still insane to me how many baby contraptions there are on the market. But beyond making sure that you have the right bottles and you are fully stocked with diapers, you want to make sure that as a parent you are in accord with your spouse or partner. You have to be on the same page about what kind of values you are instilling in your children. I almost feel like this should be a required conversation before you even think about getting married—however, I'll save that for another book.

With Jackson, we definitely took the time to have in-depth conversations about what we wanted for him in terms of his schooling, core values, and sharpening his moral compass. I felt comfortable that Devale and I were on the same page, but still, you don't know everything until that baby actually gets here and you have to learn what that specific child needs.

Anybody with more than one kid will tell you that the first

child is always the experiment. I can tell you that we were winging it with Jackson and just praying that we kept him alive. I'm glad we had a five-year head start before having our next three boys because it helped us to learn and understand that Devale and I do have different parenting styles. We also learned that how both of us were raised and our different backgrounds also played into how we interacted with our sons.

As a parent, you also have to be flexible with understanding that each child may learn differently, grow through their milestones at a different pace, and have a wildly different temperament. As they go from being toddlers to preadolescents to teenagers to young adults, there will be so many different changes. Just when you think you know your child, they will surprise you and do the very thing that you thought they would never do. As a parent, the most important thing that you have to do is practice patience because every day is going to be different.

Devale

Not only did we have to be flexible with each kid, we had to be flexible with where we were each time that we brought a new son into our home. We were living in an apartment in New York when we had Jackson. By the time we had Dakota, we were living in a single-family home the size of all the homes we *ever* lived in in Atlanta. Our socioeconomic status changed, and what we were able to provide to our sons has evolved as well. We're grateful that our sons can now grow up in a multigenerational home where they get to see their grandparents on a regular basis and not have to worry about some of the things that we struggled with when we were growing up in Brooklyn.

You learn so much from one child to the next. We quickly discovered with Jackson that we had to stay at least two to three months ahead in baby clothes because he grew so quickly. We learned how to adjust what we needed as opposed to what we wanted.

After Jackson's birth, a lot changed for us. For the first time in my life, I realized how childbirth is the closest you can get to death while still being alive. It's the most amazing miracle, but it's also terrifying to watch someone go through that journey. Jackson's birth, as scary as it was, made me realize that I had to make some changes. I knew I had to be more present with Khadeen when she came home, and I definitely had to learn more about maternal health.

My mom had me and my siblings naturally. I was nine when my sister was born, and I remember my parents bringing her home from the hospital. But my parents kept things to themselves. If my mom experienced anything afterward, she and my dad surely didn't say anything to me or my brother. With my very limited experience and exposure, I thought childbirth would be easy.

When Khadeen went into labor, I thought we were going

to have the baby, come home, and everything was going to go back to normal. But now I understand why my mom used to say, "Our bodies go through a lot as women." After watching Khadeen give birth to Jackson, my respect for women and mothers in particular went to a whole new level. After seeing it firsthand, I understood for the first time what it truly means to bring life into the world.

Part of the reason why there's a five-year gap between Jackson and Kairo is because Khadeen and I wanted to be in a better financial situation and also to discover how we were going to approach childbirth differently the second time around.

Be Present

Khadeen

Doing what we do as content creators on social media, I have to constantly remember to be more present with our sons. There was a particular afternoon when our oldest son, Jackson, came home from school and he was telling me a story about something that had happened during his day. I was focused on something else and I was not listening to him.

Jackson asked me a question in the midst of telling the story and I replied, "What'd you say, buddy?" He was frustrated and said, "But, Mommy, I just told you the whole story." I tried to refocus and said, "Okay, tell me the story again." He repeated the story and I still wasn't listening to him. Finally, he just said, "Forget it, Mommy. You're not even listening to me," and he walked away.

When he walked away, I felt so sad. Whatever I was doing in that moment wasn't more important than giving my son five minutes to focus in and hear him out. Now I admit, Jackson is very much like my brother-in-law, Brian. He tells the longest stories and you don't know when he's going to get to the point. But regardless of how long he takes to get those stories out, letting my son know that he's my priority in that moment will always take priority over any post, reel, or video that I need to put up on social media.

That moment with Jackson helped me to be more focused and to do my best to live in the moment with my boys. From the time that we began writing this book until now, my youngest son, Dakota, is already six months old. People always say that your kids grow fast—and it's true. You blink and in the next moment your kids are off to kindergarten, elementary school, middle school, high school, and then before you know it they're out of the house. I don't want to be one of those mothers who look up and say "I barely remember my son taking his first steps" or "When did he start growing a mustache?" I want to be more involved and invested in those little moments in their lives.

When Devale and I are doing our social media work, we will create a specific time for us to record our content and then as soon as we're done, we immediately put the phones away. We are always trying to do better with making sure that the kids know that even though we are showing part of our lives on social media, the cameras will not always be in their faces. We want them to know that we are actively listening to whatever it is that they want to share with us—even if it takes Jackson ten minutes to get a story out. I want my boys to know that I genuinely enjoy spending time with them.

Before I had kids, I would definitely say that I did my best work at the last minute. But after being a mama to these boys for the last eleven years, it's a totally different story because they are quick to call me out if I forget something. Without fail, I will hear "But, Mommy, you promised me!" or "Mommy, you said we were gonna do this before dinner!" Making sure that I am more cognizant of what I say to my boys has made me more efficient and forces me to stay on track.

Devale

One morning Khadeen and I had an argument before I took Jackson to school. We typically try to do our best not to argue in front of the boys, but we had to keep moving out the door and get him to school on time. Most mornings, we have a pretty smooth routine where we listen to *The Breakfast Club* and I talk to him about his day while we're driving in the car, and when he gets out, Jackson and I will share our special handshake before he enters the building. But this day I was very quiet during the drive to school, and didn't put on the radio. I know in particular for me I was trying to keep my cool so I could regroup from the argument. My focus at that moment was to get him to school safely and on time, then get back to the house so we could finish our discussion and get to the other side of it.

We were already running late because of the argument so when we finally pulled up, Jackson and I didn't get to do our handshake. He turned around and said, "But, Daddy, we didn't get to do our handshake." I said, "I know, buddy, but you gotta get to school." He gave me this sad look, jumped out the car, and walked into the building.

Khadeen and I went on about our day, we resolved our argument, and in my mind everything was good. When I returned later on in the afternoon to pick up Jackson from school, I was surprised because he was one of the last kids to walk out of the building. Typically, when I pick him up, he's running at full speed and jumps into my arms. That afternoon he looked like he had lost his best friend. I said, "What's wrong?" He looked at me and said, "Daddy, are you still mad at me?"

That shit hit me like a ton of bricks in the nuts. At that point, all I could think was, "Wow! I am the worst person in the world." I only have one job as a parent—and that's to make sure that my children are prepared to be as successful and productive as they can be. I felt awful that my son had been walking around in school for six hours thinking, "What did I do to make Daddy so mad at me?" Jackson is a sensitive kid in general, but I was hurt because I knew that the argument had had nothing to do with him. But he didn't have the emotional tools yet to know that that moment wasn't about him and that it wasn't his fault.

That incident helped me to realize that I had to learn how to not project my thoughts, feelings, and emotions onto other people, especially my sons. One thing that I've realized now that I have four boys is that I have to be very careful of the energies I bring into our household.

I've learned that when I walk into the house, I am not going to bring the outside world into my home because my kids have nothing to do with that. No matter how upset I am about my gym, my agent, my manager, my family, or whatever else is going on outside, when I come into the house I'm going to have a smile on my face and I'm going to let the children receive me with that energy.

When I used to walk in after having a bad day, I noticed the kids would be very quiet. I would hear them whispering in the kitchen, "Mommy, what's wrong with Daddy?" I now realize as their father and as their male role model, I set the tone for how we will operate energetically in our home as a family. What I demonstrate to my sons today will carry forward into their future when they become husbands and create families of their own. I don't want any of my future daughters-in-law coming back to me and being frustrated because my sons don't know how to properly manage their emotions. As I learn each day to manage my energy and how I project myself out into the world, I'm always conscious that I am setting the standard for my sons to be able to walk in my footsteps.

Parenting While Black

Khadeen

There is nothing more nerve-racking than being a mother to four young Black boys. Of course I thank God for blessing me with my sons. But the way that my anxiety is set up, it's challenging at times to have peace and not to worry about them. Clearly God knows best and he knows that I can handle it, but it does rattle my nerves to think about raising four young Black men in a country where they will be systemically preyed upon before they even know what's happening.

For so many Black parents throughout the country, particularly in the summer of 2020, most of us were forced to have "The Talk" with them about the realities of being young Black men in this country and how to conduct and protect themselves. All my sons wanted to do that summer was to be kids and run around and play. But we knew with all the imagery that was coming through television and social media, we couldn't just pretend like we could shield our sons from the reality of who they were as young Black boys and who they would eventually become as Black men. The images that I saw during that summer and continue to see in this present moment affected me, so I knew that Devale and I had to be proactive about having an authentic discussion with them, even with our son Kaz, who was only three at the time.

It was like that summer forced us to have that conversation with our sons and unfortunately it meant that we had to strip a little of their innocence away from them. While it was difficult to do that, especially with all our boys being under the age of ten at the time, one thing that Devale and I have agreed upon as parents is to always be transparent with our sons. That was probably one of the most difficult conversations we've ever had to have in this household because I saw firsthand how it affected them. But as things continue to happen in the world that we have no control over, I always want to make sure that my sons hear firsthand from me what's happening around them so that they can be well equipped and know that our home is a refuge for them.

Devale

It's a simple fact that Black people have to raise their kids differently than the rest of America. I've had people say to me that Khadeen and I are parenting our boys the wrong way. Not that I give much energy to social media critics in the first place, but as a Black father I don't have the leeway to allow my sons to go out into the world and make the same kind of mistakes as their white peers. Their mistakes could cost them their lives or put them behind bars. This is not just an opinion, this is a fact. Black men and women from the time they are children are punished and sentenced at a much higher rate for the same infractions than any other racial group in the country.

Preparing them for the real world and ensuring that they are well rounded and compassionate young men is a fine line that is still hard to navigate, even with having more than a decade of fatherhood under my belt. I want my sons to be strong, tough, and resilient. I also want them to be comfortable knowing when it is okay to cry in public, show emotion, and let people know when they are hurt. So often there aren't enough spaces in this country for Black kids to experience compassion and empathy. I know as a father that I lean more on wanting my boys to be more resilient than emotional. But even with the harsh realities that I know they are going to face, I also want them to have good hearts. I want them to grow into strong Black men who can eventually become strong Black husbands.

KHADEEN'S HOT TAKE

Make Your Heart and Home a Refuge

One of the most important things that I always want to establish with my sons is making sure that they know that our home is a place of refuge for them. It's not a place to be enabled. It's not a place for them to stay indefinitely without a game plan. But when they need a soft and compassionate place to be, I want them to know that the first place they can run to is home to wherever Devale and I are. Particularly with us raising young Black sons, there aren't always enough spaces for young Black children to be vulnerable about who they are and what they're feeling. At the end of the day, I want my sons to know that no matter who they grow up to be, my heart and my home are always going to be a place where they can find love.

Without fail, our kids are going to make mistakes as they get out there into the world and discover who they are. But one thing I would encourage you to do is to have frequent and open communications with your children to let them know that there is a safe place for them to land when the world hits them up with those bruises and scrapes. Now I ain't telling you to let your kids stay in your house for months and years on end. But particularly if you're a Black parent and you know your kid is trying to do the right thing, create that space in your home where they can take refuge and know that they have the courage to get back up and try it again.

Sometimes You Gotta Tag Yourself Out!

Khadeen

Now that we have four boys, I gotta be real careful about falling into mommy guilt and feeling like I will never be able to do enough for each child. I often have to check myself and realize that I still have to take care of Khadeen, the woman, and make sure that my needs don't fall out of the mix. I'm glad that Devale and I have a system where we can just look at each other and say, "Yo, tag me out!" We can tell when the other needs some time. Sometimes I'll ask him to take all four kids and do an activity in another room or to call another family member so I can sleep, think, or just go to the bathroom in peace. Sometimes I need that. It's very necessary to have the time away to be able to recharge. As Devale and I continue to focus on building our legacy for our boys, we have to be able to take that time away to regroup, generate income, and make sure we are the best version of who we can be for ourselves and for them.

We know how fortunate we are to have a strong village of people around us who are willing to take our children and who we know will love on them just as much as we do. We couldn't do any of this without our families. Creating our podcast, running our social media, and even writing this book wouldn't be possible without our village. As working parents, it's hard to get in that quality time without grand-parents, aunties and uncles, and extended family members who don't mind showing up so that you can get that "me" time.

Sometimes you can be so focused on preparing the best life for your kids that you don't realize as a parent that you also have to create the best life for yourself. Don't be afraid to ask for help and space. If your village isn't nearby, be honest with your partner and tag yourself out and go sit in the bath-room by yourself for fifteen to twenty minutes. Go take a walk around the block. Whatever it is, don't get so burned out that you are afraid to ask for what you need. I frequently get asked about balance, particularly when I am speaking in mommy forums. I honestly believe that I do a terrible job of balancing things. Though I may seem to have it all together, I usually don't. Balance literally does not exist. I feel like I need to sometimes allow the chips to fall where they may, reset, and reprioritize. As women, especially mothers, we usually want to do everything on our own. It may be in part because we feel like we do it best, or we may be particular about how certain tasks are completed. I have learned that divide and conquer is a whole lot more efficient than juggling and dropping the balls because one thing about them balls, they gon' drop. Being proactive and delegating responsibilities or learning when to solicit help is way more effective than having to be reactive when things don't go as planned or are incomplete. Kids are usually pretty resilient and will roll with the punches as long as there is a routine in place. Grace, girl—grace. She and I have become very acquainted.

Devale

In addition to investing money for your future, it is also important to invest money in the present so that you can get away with your spouse or partner and keep the romance going. You don't want to lose sight of each other because you're so focused on the kids. Your spouse is going to feel that, and your kids are going to feel it, too. I've learned that the more kids you have, the more important it is to put some money aside and say, "We need a babysitter for three or four hours every Friday. Let's put that in our budget." You have to find a way to tag yourself out because it's important for your mental health and your ability to be with your children when they need you.

This is specifically for the men: After you have children, understand that your life is going to change. Your wife is going to change, and don't expect that when the baby comes that things will go back to the way they used to be. Once you leave the hospital, that's when things get real. Especially if your wife or girlfriend decides to breastfeed. Now you're going to have at least another six months of her having to be up every two and a half hours to nurse, and sleep deprivation is very real. That lack of rest is going to create some very real emotional highs and lows for her. As men, we have to step up and help them cope through that. The most important thing for us not to do during this time is to panic. Take the time to find that groove with your spouse or partner so that you know how to take turns caring for your child. If one of you is better at diaper changing, step up and do that. If you're good at making the voices during the nighttime stories, make sure you're there for bedtime. Give yourself the grace to figure out what kind of parents you both want to be and allow yourself to take a break as needed.

Getting on the Same Page

Khadeen

Fortunately, Devale and I align on many of our core parenting beliefs. We both believe it's important to have honest and transparent conversations with our sons. We believe it's important to set a good example for them about what a good relationship looks like. However, we do have different styles and approaches to how we handle things with the boys. I may have to do something different with Jackson because he is the oldest than I would do with Kairo and Kaz. We are still discovering who Dakota is, so he might throw us some curveballs that we haven't experienced yet with our oldest three. You just never know as a parent!

It's a learning curve with these boys all the time. I lean on Devale a lot and I believe we are complementary in how we feed off each other. With Devale being the father, I do allow him to take the lead on some things because he was once a boy himself and he can directly share those personal experiences with our sons. I am completely open when Devale needs to say, "Don't just jump on them for that because boys tend to act like this." We're also not afraid to pull each other aside and say, "I think you should've done this differently" or "I think you need to have this discussion a different way."

I also think it's equally important to apologize to your child when you know that you've done something wrong. I know that most of you reading this book grew up in a similar way to me and Devale in the "Do as I Say and Don't Question Me" generation with your parents. Trust me, the last thing I would ever dream of doing growing up in a Caribbean household would be talking back to my parents after they gave me explicit instructions. But I believe there's a lot of power in taking the time to talk with your children and apologize to them when it's necessary.

We are very vocal with our sons about why we parent and discipline them the way we do. I believe every parent shouldn't be afraid to say to their child, "Mommy did not make the best decision," "Mommy apologizes for the way she handled that," or "Mommy was upset in the moment and I should not have said that."

We should handle our children with the same kind of respect that we would give to another adult, because then it keeps the lines of communication open. I am proud that we have given our sons the space to feel open to say what they need to say to us and I always want to make sure that they feel comfortable in sharing whatever it is in their hearts.

It's beautifully mind-blowing and insanely scary when you see some of your or your spouse's qualities and characteristics exhibited in your children. Particularly the qualities that you are not so fond of within yourself. The qualities that you know you need to work on for the betterment of yourself and your future. Then you add the layer of a husband who is super to-the-point and blunt and tells you that you cannot reprimand your son for the same behavior you exhibit. Ouch! Talk about being put on front street and then feeling guilty for trying to correct a behavior in your child that you have lived out most of your life.

But I think the issue that arises for me in this circumstance is that I'm trying to get my children out of the bad habits that I so desperately am trying to break as an adult. I immediately try to break my kids of behaviors that may have prohibited me from advancing in an area of my life if I see them. Some may be innate, others possibly genetic, but some are definitely learned behaviors that I feel can be corrected if trained from a young age. It can be a bruise to the ego when your spouse tells you that your child is doing some thing that you often complain about yourself or have been called out on. There's no ego in parenting. And the sooner you own up to the fact that you are not perfect, then you can be on your road to becoming the perfect parent for your child.

Devale

Before becoming a father, I had a little bit more experience dealing with boys because I ran a mentorship program for young men, from ages six through twenty-two. I had gotten into the rhythm of not only dealing with boys through my own personal experiences but also through seeing how these boys interacted with their own fathers. But even with that experience, you don't know how you are going to deal with situations until you have children of your own and have to solve problems in real time.

Khadeen and I don't wait to have a family caucus the way that my parents did. If something happens with one of our boys in the moment, we tackle it head-on and make sure that they're not walking around all day feeling confused or upset because we haven't taken the adequate time to break something down for them.

If I'm not there and there's an issue with homework, Khadeen will jump in and then we'll discuss later what happened. If she's not there, I will do the same thing. I think this works well for us because we're always bouncing ideas off each other and we take the time to do a lot of reflection about how our choices are impacting our boys every day. I'll ask her sometimes, "Do you think I was a little too hard?" or "Was I a little too soft about that?"

We definitely spend every night—and I do mean every night—recapping what happened with our sons throughout the day. We check in with each other frequently because we want them to respect both of us, even if one of us is not in the room. I don't ever want it to be a thing where my boys think, "Daddy's not here, so I know I can get over on Mommy" or "Mommy's not here, so I know I can do this because Daddy's watching us."

If you really want to parent and parent well, the first thing you need to do is look back into how you were raised and evaluate what you do—and, most important, what you *do not*—want to pass forward to your children. You got people out here parenting a certain way and passing on their trauma to their children and being completely unaware of what they're doing. Just because something has always been done in your family doesn't mean it was always the right way. You have to learn why it was done that way so that you have a purposeful reason to continue—or discontinue—a tradition or practice with your children. Using tradition as an excuse is a lazy way to parent. Times and circumstances have changed, and you owe it to yourself as a parent and you owe it to your children to look at them for who they are and to give them the time, tools, and love that will work best for them.

Conclusion

Building Legacy,
Loyalty, and Peace

We hope that you have enjoyed taking this journey with us. It takes time and patience to discover what qualities and values go into the foundation of your relationship. Choosing to be in a loving, committed, long-term relationship is not for the faint of heart—and then (at least for us) adding four kids and a few businesses on top of that requires even more heart and just a little bit of crazy to make it from one day to the next.

But when you find out what makes your relationship work, it's worth every argument and reconciliation, every breakdown and breakthrough, and every breakup and make-up. When your arguments get a little shorter and that blow-out diaper or leaking ceiling doesn't make you consider divorce, you know that you are doing the work to take your love to the distance—and beyond.

By this final chapter, you know that we still don't have the answers for you. But we hope that you've seen through our journey that good love takes friendship, grace, and service. If we can get through an abortion, bankruptcy, infidelity, and near-death experiences, or whatever you are facing in your relationship, you can do it, too. Every day is an opportunity to write a new page in your love story. And even if you're standing in the middle of an unexpected plot twist, we hope that we've inspired you to know that when you're with the right person, they are worth turning the page and finding your way to your own definition of happily ever after.

Devale

During the first five years of our marriage, Khadeen and I were struggling big time. We talked about divorce numerous times, but we couldn't agree on how to do life together without being married, so divorce no longer became an option. One day in particular, Khadeen and I were in one of our local gyms arguing. At the time, I was working a minimum of fourteen hours a day every day to ensure we had everything we needed. I was balancing three businesses, working as a color commentator for MSG Varsity, running to the city for commercial auditions, at least three times a week, and still personal training for extra cash. Kay had slowed down from work because we both decided it would be better for Jackson if she was more present at home.

Kay was just coming off her thirtieth birthday and made

a pledge to herself to be in the best shape of her life before we started to try for another baby. We were making more money but I was still nervous about our financial situation because it took us seven years to recover from the recession, and I vowed never to be back in that situation again. Meanwhile, it was the top of the year and Kay and I were fresh off an argument about the AmEx bill from Christmas. This day she walked in the gym around six o'clock. Three hours passed, and it was now a few minutes before nine. I was ready to go and she hadn't worked out yet.

I remember saying, "Man, you haven't worked out yet, and you've already been here a while. Why are you being so lazy?"

"I'm not being lazy. I just don't feel good."

This sparked an argument. At this point, I was making more than enough money to support our family and give us some financial freedom so that Khadeen didn't have to work. I was a little bit perplexed as to why she would be tired. I was exhausted from the day and the countless disagreements about everything. My tone was a bit harsh and Kay was giving it right back to me.

I said, "We might need to think about getting a divorce if we can't have conversations with each other without it becoming a screaming match. Here we are in public, and I got to close the door to this gym because you and I are constantly arguing about everything. This is just too much! You are not putting in the work, you're just fucking lazy."

Khadeen screamed back at me, "I'm not fucking lazy, Devale. I'm fucking pregnant. I was trying to keep it a secret until I could tell you in a special way, but I didn't know how to do it. Here you are talking about getting a divorce and I'm pregnant."

I was embarrassed. I sat there for a hot second as all the air left the room. All I could say was, "*Well, why didn't you start with that?* I didn't know that you were pregnant. I didn't understand why you were so tired, emotional, and incapable of having a sane conversation. You have to communicate to me what's going on so I know how to respond to your responses, woman."

We sat there together in my gym office quiet for about thirty seconds, and then we began laughing.

I couldn't fathom doing life without Khadeen. There's no word that describes what Khadeen is to me. Best friend isn't enough. Soulmate isn't enough. Wife isn't enough. Khadeen and I literally built a life from the time we were eighteen years old, and we built it together. There is no doing life without Khadeen. Every moment I've had as an adult has been with Khadeen.

Describing Khadeen as my soulmate is a disservice to the connection we have. I don't think there is a word created by humans that can describe how Khadeen and I work together. It's so far beyond a sexual, physical, mental, emotional, or spiritual connection. It's bigger than just making money and building an empire together. It's creating a safe space for our children. It's creating a legacy that's going to last for our children's children. I want my grandchildren to be able to look back and say, "My grandparents didn't follow everyone else's plan on what a marriage, a friendship, or a relationship is supposed to be. They did it their way!"

We don't owe anybody out here anything. We're all out here guessing about what life is supposed to be. I'm tired of trying to guess what other people are going to say my life should be. I'm going to create my life the way I want to, and I want to create it with this woman right here. I know that this is what works for me and this is what's been working for us. I don't plan on ever losing it because this is the only thing that brings me peace. When you have something worth fighting for, I hope that you, too, will do the work to discover and maintain what will bring the most peace, security, and longevity in your relationship.

DEVALE'S HOT TAKE
Busting Up the Alpha Male Myth

One of the things we have to do as men is bust up this whole idea of what we think an alpha man is. Being an alpha male doesn't mean that you control your wife or the woman you are in a relationship with. Becoming a true alpha male means that you control everything that exists around her so that she can do the things that she wants to do. That's a big difference. The whole idea of being an alpha male and controlling your wife shows a huge insecurity.

It's my job and my joy as a husband to create the conditions where Khadeen can go out and fulfill her heart's desire. And that's not just about what's in our bank account—it's also about me making sure that our boys are well taken care of and that Khadeen has the time to rest, recover, and do the personal and professional things in her life that make her feel like a woman. I love that she is creating her own businesses and partnering with people and brands to be an influence on the things that she cares about. Seeing her fulfill her dreams is more important to me than just feeling the need to dominate her.

Khadeen

Early on in our marriage, around the five-year mark, we were having a rough patch and it was another moment that I felt like I could lose him. Devale and I were battling with seeking attention outside of our marriage. We were both in a selfish place at the time. I felt like I was just existing within this marriage. I was not confident in who I was as a wife. I was feeling inadequate. Part of it was not having a grasp on juggling being a wife and a new mom. There were just so many things that I had going on that I felt overwhelmed.

My feeling of being overwhelmed led me to entertain somebody else outside of my marriage. In that moment I felt like I would lose my husband, and at the end of the day, it wasn't worth it. I was seeking entertainment from somebody else because it felt good in the moment to escape. I remember thinking, "Wow, I could change the entire trajectory of my marriage by doing something so stupid." That experience required me to go back to what had attracted me to Devale in the first place. I started reminiscing about the things that initially drew us together and that we initially loved to do for each other. I eventually realized that everything that I ever wanted and desired was in Devale.

To be honest, we both were checked out to a certain extent. It's hard to pinpoint now what exactly kept us fighting to stay together. Part of it was our commitment to Jackson because we owed it to that child to be the best versions of ourselves and to raise him in a two-parent household. But we also knew that being miserable was not going to benefit him either. Not being on one accord made us miserable. We were still in the same book, but we were definitely in different chapters.

We needed to refocus on each other. That moment really took me back to the starting point of asking myself, "What do I need from Devale?" and "What does Devale need from me?" I took the time to really focus on those things. I knew that we ultimately loved each other and couldn't live our lives without each other. We had to just drown out all the other extra distractions.

I had to take the onus on myself to say, "Khadeen, you're not doing all the things that you should be doing for this man. You're also not doing all the things that you should be doing for yourself." When I look back on it, I was probably mildly depressed, too, because I felt like I was in a rut. When you're at that sacrificial point of life, when you're in that building phase of life, you just feel like you're doing a lot of the same stuff over and over again.

I think we were both ready to get to the next level in our lives and have more autonomy over our time and our life. It was a matter of finding a way to stay connected while we were hustling, juggling Jackson, and still trying to figure out how we were going to get out of our apartment one day.

These are all the things we were working toward on a daily basis that did not seem tangible in that moment. I think that's what happens with a lot of people. You get caught in the monotony of your life and you lose sight of the bigger picture. You lose sight of what it is you really want. Once Devale and I refocused and we really talked about how much better we were together than we were apart, that's when I think things took a turn for us. We realized we wanted more children. We wanted more as a family and we wanted more for ourselves as a couple. And when we took that time to refocus, our second son, Kairo, came shortly after that.

Validate Your Own Relationship

Devale

If you are on the verge of a breakup, you have to ask yourself: Are you considering ending your relationship because of what's actually happening in your relationship, or are you breaking down because of other people's opinions about your relationship? Far too often people find themselves as the objects of someone else's projection. When you listen to too many outside opinions, you will find yourself feeling bad or anxious about something in your relationship that was never an issue for you in the first place.

If someone else is telling you that you should feel a certain way about a situation in your relationship, you have to ask yourself, "Is it worth me losing the person I love over an opinion that is not my own?" Human beings are going to project their ideas onto other people without even realizing it. We all do it every day without being conscious that we are placing expectations and ideals on to one another. We have to start looking for happiness and peace within. We can't keep looking at other people for answers to our life.

We've all been born with one inalienable right—and that's to survive by any means necessary. When you start to look within yourself and stop seeking answers for your life from outside sources, you'll realize that the answers are always within. Same thing with your relationship. Seek answers for how you feel, what you want, what you need from yourself and from your partner. Constantly seeking affirmation and answers from people outside is only going to lead to confusion and, most important, heartache.

Khadeen

Hollywood has such a great way of glamorizing everything, including thinking patterns, ideas, and behaviors that are dangerous for marriages. Be aware of the shows you are watching repeatedly. Do not let their ideas and desires eventually become yours—especially when it comes to how you treat your husband or wife. Other people's projections can never become your reality because social media is not a real place and those folks in the comments are usually the loud minority.

If Devale and I are committed to building a life together, what point does it make to ask other people or accept other people's opinions about how we are going to get to that goal? At times it does help to share. How many times have you felt like you were the only one dealing with a particular struggle? Did you find some relief when you realized that you weren't the only person experiencing it? I'm not referring to this as a "misery loves company" kind of comradery, but more like thank goodness I'm not dealing with something so extremely far-fetched. We're the only ones that have to live our everyday lives. Other people can suggest things, but they really can't help. When you start to use other people as a barometer for your happiness, their projections eerily find a way of infiltrating your system.

For the couple who is going through it and trying to find their sweet spot again, you have to do the work to know if you're willing to fight for your relationship. I often joke that Devale and I have been divorced and remarried at least five times within our relationship over the last twenty years. Those breakups and make-ups have been during different phases in our relationship, whether it was in college, a couple of years into our marriage, or even last week. But one thing that Devale and I have is a strong need for each other and a desire to see each other win. Devale is my best friend before anything else. The thought of not having him as my friend literally guts me.

Early on in our marriage, I would argue and debate just to get my point across. It wasn't about being right, but I had to express to Devale how I arrived at a particular action. Most of the time, he never even cared about my reasoning behind things. Instead of arguing him down, I had to learn to listen to the way he received what I said and focus on his reception versus telling him my side of the story.

So many people cannot see themselves honestly enough to say "I might have been wrong in this circumstance. Let me not take this personally," or be courageous enough to ask, "How can I adjust my behavior accordingly?"

Devale and I can have a disagreement and be in the middle of a heated argument. I will straight up not like him after we're done. But at the end of the day, he's my homie and we're going to work to come to an agreement for ourselves and our family. If you are going through a hard time and you can't seem to agree on how to move forward, take it back to the foundation of your friendship. What is the root of your relationship? What are you willing to fight and strive for together? How did it all start? People always say communication is the key to a great relationship, but when you are going through a rough season, listening is equally important.

One time a few years ago, we were not seeing eye to eye on a couple of things. I felt like I desperately needed to bring us back to a space where we both could be reminded of our why and how it all started. So I told him to get in the car and we went for a drive. The road led back to Hofstra University, where this all started. Once he realized where we were, he grabbed my hand, smiled at me, and said, "I see what you're doing here." We drove past Hofstra and parked in the same spot that his car was parked in when I walked out of that charity event back on October 3, 2002, and met him for our first date. I then drove over to the student center where we got the infamous hero, chips, and pickles—a meal that forever changed my life. I drove past each of the dormitories that I lived in during our time at Hofstra. From my single room at 912 Estabrook Hall, to my suite in Nassau, and then on to my apartment at Colonial Square, this was a reminder of the times that we shared when things were so simple. There were no bills, no children, no real responsibility—we were just two kids with an insanely strong connection and affinity for each other.

"Take care of me, so I can take care of us," Devale would say early on in our relationship. It's a motto that stuck with us, even to this day. It's important for us to show that our marriage is a whole system of reciprocity. When I take care of Devale, I know that he is taking care of me. My goal is always to provide a home life for Devale where he's comfortable and he knows that he can let go of the weight of the world. He should be able to walk through these doors and unload, with the vulnerability to fall into my arms knowing that this is home. This is your refuge, your safe space. With that firm foundation in place, he can then strategize how he's going to continue to build a legacy for us and for our sons.

The Love You Build Today Creates Your Family's Legacy for Tomorrow

Khadeen

When we were sharing a twin-size bed in college when I lived in the Nassau suites at Hofstra, Devale and I would look up at the ceiling as we lay together in a sweet, comforting silence. Then he would whisper to me, "I can't wait till we get our dream home one day, fill it with kids, and you wake up in our king-size bed beaming with excitement because we are living the life!" We had several moments like this in our apartment back in Brooklyn, too. With every moment of ascension, there was gratitude for the present but hope for the future. And here we are—a dream turned reality. An answered prayer. I recently saw a meme on social media that read "You are now living in one of the prayers that you've prayed for throughout your life." Devale and I have continuously prayed for and talked about our life goals throughout our relationship. The same two college kids who innocently fell in love over the student cafe heroes and talked for hours on the first linkup are now grown-ups with four beautiful boys. The hopes and dreams that left our lips very early on were indeed manifestations of a life we not only dreamed of but were willing to work for diligently.

There is a relentlessness that we have individually and collectively that we can attribute to how we build our present-day life. It's really amazing and humbling to see so many of the same things that were merely a thought or aspiration, we are experiencing and living in now. There are so many moments where I almost have an out-of-body experience. I look at each of my boys while at home in the family room, playing and loving on one another with me nestled in Devale's embrace on the couch, and I stop to thank God for His favor and faithfulness. No matter the obstacle, I'm so grateful and in awe of how we've been able to stay the course despite the obstacles that came our way.

Devale and I tend to focus on our short-term goals within the span of a year and we also look out toward our five- and ten-year goals. These goals give us direction, foster focus, and are a constant reminder of our why. Aside from Jackson, Kairo, Kaz, and Dakota, our purpose provides a reason to get up in the morning and do what we need to—even during the moments of exhaustion. This strategy has worked for us for the past twenty years. There is nothing like doing life with your best friend and having someone who is constantly pouring into your mind, heart, and soul.

Everyone should have a trusted sounding board to bounce ideas off. This person should be honest, willing to be an active listener, give sound advice when needed, and most importantly, be worthy of being privy to your deepest thoughts and desires. Not everyone deserves access to your wildest dreams, so protect yourself and guard your heart. Some of my favorite times with Devale are when we stumble upon open and honest conversation about what's new. It can be while getting ready for bed at night, during a date night, or a late-night moment after getting the kids in bed. I love when he and I can reflect and say "I can't believe this opportunity is happening right now!" or "How do you think we can go about doing this new thing next year?" Giving ourselves the space to bounce ideas off each other without judgment or cynicism has been the biggest help. After all, two heads are usually better than one—if it's the right head of course. I love moments where I can say "Wow! I didn't even think of that!" when setting a plan in motion or navigating through an idea. We help each other map out how those things are going to happen and love to see how it becomes feasible for us.

Now that we're done having children, I'm focused on what I need to do to balance my life as a mother of four, wife, and career woman. I'm prioritizing what I need to do to get myself and my goals back on track. I've had moments where I question what my purpose is here on Earth. At times, I've felt that it needed to be some grandiose mantra that can eloquently roll off my lips when asked. Then I've had times where I felt like I didn't need to announce my purpose because that was on a need-to-know basis, and folks didn't necessarily need to know. One thing I do know for certain, much of my purpose is woven into the fabric of who I am and my success as a mother and wife. How I show up daily for my family is of utmost importance to me. Going back to the introduction, I've fantasized about the life that I am currently living. My groom now has a face—and a perfect one at that. My children are the quintessential combinations of the best parts of Devale and I. I am in a position to assist my family in ways I've always wanted to. My family deserves what I'm able to provide, especially after all the sacrifice they've made over the course of my life. While I enjoy planning for the future, my priority is to be present in the times that really matter, especially with my boys. I don't want to miss a thing. My energy has shifted into taking care of myself so I can show up wholly for my family. And to be truthful, there are moments when I'm ready to completely log off from social media for good—disable the YouTube page and uninstall Instagram and Facebook. But then I get a reminder from someone who supports our journey, has been rooting for my family and myself, or shares a testimony about how sharing our story has helped to inspire them. Getting a "you guys helped save my marriage" makes my heart smile. That keeps me going and is so appreciated. I guess we can add that to my purpose—living a life that shows others that anything is possible as long as you move with love in your hearts, continue to pay it forward to others, and bless others around you in the process. None of this is just for me. When your calling is higher and you live in abundance, it is your duty to make sure that others around you are okay. And lastly, while doing all the things, take a note from my late paternal grandmother and take everything "one day at a time."

Devale

There have been points in my marriage where I thought I couldn't do it anymore. But as I have matured, I now understand that having those thoughts is normal. It's how you choose to act on those thoughts that will show you if you are in the right place or not. These thoughts still come from time to time, because everyone in this house is still learning how to manage their desires, But then I take a step back and I think about Khadeen, and then I think about Jackson, Kairo, Kaz, and Dakota. I get over myself and my ego and I start thinking about what's important for them. Khadeen has been my best friend and business partner for almost two decades now. We've worked our asses off to develop a brand and business model that works for us and creates a strong legacy for our kids. We've built a friendship that I am absolutely confident will outlast anything. I'm confident in the strength of our relationship because when we were flat broke, we were still the best of friends and we always found ways to enjoy our lives, even during the harshest of times. I never want to give that up.

My legacy is not just about me. It's about supporting and loving my best friend, growing my boys into productive members of society, and showing other couples that it is possible to have a loving, supportive, and enduring marriage—and have a whole lot of fun doing it!

Acknowledgments

First and foremost, we would like to thank God for every moment given to both of us on this journey called life together and during this creative process.

To my Kay Kay, thank you so much for trusting me with everything, from your heart to your goals. You have been my motivation, my muse, and my place of peace for twenty years and counting. I love you and will forever honor you as my partner— my ride or die.

To Devale, my love, my everything. Boy oh boy, did God take his time on you. My most perfect person—who could have predicted how our lives would unfold together. I'm so grateful! Every high, every low, every win, and every loss have all worked together for our good. Loving and living life with you will always be my most favorite thing to do. I love you *this* much!

To our children, Jackson, Kairo, Kaz, and Dakota. You guys will forever be the greatest accomplishments we created together. We thank God for you daily and pray that our imperfections and shortcomings as parents and individuals will serve as both life lessons and laughable little moments that you can share with your children in the future. We love you guys so much!

To my parents, Troy and Karen, obviously there is no me without you guys. But more importantly, this version of me only exists because of your sacrifice and purpose-driven love. You guys encouraged me to dream, while holding me accountable as the only person that can make my dreams come true. You both will forever be the wind beneath my wings (lol that quote was for you Ma).

To Mom and Dad—from humble beginnings in Jamaica and St. Vincent, respectively, to migrating to New York to advance yourselves and your families. I am constantly in awe of your journeys and bravery over the years. Your unyielding dedication, hard work, sacrifices, and love for me have been the driving force behind the woman I am today. Thank you for loving and supporting me relentlessly. I promise to always strive to make you proud!

To our manager, Dinorah Peña, and the team at Bodega7—*you're amazing*! With you there is nothing we can't do. We think it . . . We speak it . . . We make it happen! It's the Brooklyn way. Love you immensely.

To our publishing team: thank you Carlos Segarra at

Creative Artists Agency; our editor, Michele Eniclerico, and art director, Anna Bauer, at Penguin Random House; our attorney, Dr. Keith White, Esq., for always believing in us and affirming that this is only the beginning. We love you greatly.

To Leah Lakins, words cannot express what you've been able to do with our thoughts and our words. You were patient, you were kind, and you were brilliant with this process. Thank you for working around our busy schedules and noise and exhausting Zoom calls. May God bless you and continue to keep you.

Let's keep choosing love over everything else!

About the Authors

DEVALE ELLIS is a former NFL player turned actor known for his lead roles on Tyler Perry's *Sistas* and the spin-off based on his character, *Zatima*. He is the cocreator, along with Khadeen, of a viral social sitcom on YouTube and Facebook, *The Ellises,* and cohost of the Webby Award–winning podcast, *Dead Ass with Khadeen and Devale Ellis.*

KHADEEN ELLIS is a TV host and actress. She is a two-season alum of OWN's *Black Love* docuseries, has made appearances on Tyler Perry's *Bruh* and BET's *Bigger,* and has served as a speaker at conferences such as Essence Festival and The Momference. The Ellises podcast, *Dead Ass,* covers life, love, sex, and marriage, with notable guests, including President Joe Biden.